PETER OF SPAIN

TRACTATUS SYNCATEGOREMATUM

AND SELECTED ANONYMOUS TREATISES

MEDIAEVAL PHILOSOPHICAL TEXTS IN TRANSLATION
No. 13

Marquette University Press
1131 W. Wisconsin Ave.
Milwaukee, Wisconsin

PETER OF SPAIN

TRACTATUS SYNCATEGOREMATUM

AND SELECTED ANONYMOUS TREATISES

Translated

By

JOSEPH P. MULLALLY, Ph.D.
ASSOCIATE PROFESSOR OF PHILOSOPHY
QUEENS COLLEGE, FLUSHING, N.Y.

With an Introduction

By

Joseph P. Mullally, Ph.D.

and

Roland Houde, Ph.D.
Professor of Philosophy
Université de Montréal, Montréal, Canada

MARQUETTE UNIVERSITY PRESS   MILWAUKEE, WIS.   1964

Library of Congress Catalog Card Number: 64-17335

© Copyright, 1964, The Marquette University Press

Milwaukee, Wisconsin

Manufactured in the United States of America

vi

Dedicated To
Professor Ernest A. Moody
and
Daniel D. Flanagan
with deepest gratitude

CONTENTS

Introduction

THE HISTORY OF LOGIC

At the very outset the point must be re-emphasized that the history of logic, just like the history of philosophy, is dependent upon faithful translations and critical editions. It is and must remain a matter of concern that a satisfactory history of logic is still to be written. The last century of scholarship in logic has produced historical outlines and anthologies which are far from presenting a fair conspectus of any school or period of logic. In 1838, Adolphe Franck published his *Esquisse d'une histoire de la logique précédée d'une analyse étendue de l'Organum d'Aristote.*[1] This sketch pays more attention to the analytic survey of the *Organon* than to its historical influence through the Middle Ages. As a matter of fact, Peter of Spain is not even mentioned in the work. Franck's emphasis on Lullian logic[2] is acknowledgedly derived from the *Histoire de la logique*[3] of Pierre Gassendi (1592-1655). As for Robert Blakey's *Historical Sketch of Logic, from the Earliest Times to the Present,*[4] one notices again that the influence of Peter of Spain and his *Summulae Logicales* is not singled out, while the task—characteristic of our century—of recognizing a strict formal logic is dismissed in quite a cavalier way:

> the logical philosophy of the scholastic ages is closely identified with mental science itself; so much so, indeed, that it becomes a difficult task to keep always in view the radical distinction between that science, and the purely dialectic forms or systems which are ever obtruded on our notice in the abstract speculations of the Middle Ages.[5]

Dissatisfaction with Prantl's *Geschichte der Logik im Abendland*[6] has been voiced clearly. The shortcomings of this history can be classified under two main headings: (a) ignorance of or lack of appreciation of unedited logic manuscripts,[7] and (b) a reduction of logic to or a confusion of logic with the problem of universals.[8] The research of

---

[1] (Paris: Hachette), pp. 1 to 188 cover the systematic study; the history proper runs from p. 189 to p. 308.

[2] Raymond Lull (1235-1315).

[3] Tome I of Gassendi's *Opera Omnia* (Lugdunum: Sumptibus Lavrentii Anisson & Ioan. Bapt. Devenet, 1658).

[4] (London: H. Baillière, 1851), pp. 493-524 contain a bibliography of logic.

[5] *Ibid.,* p. 121.

[6] (Leipzig: S. Hirzel, 1855-1870); (1955 Reprint—Graz, Austria: Akademische Druck-U Verlagsanstalt, 4 vols. in 3 vols., 1,906 pp.)

[7] Martin Grabmann, *Bearbeitungen und Auslegungen der aristotelischen Logik aus der Zeit von Peter Abaelard bis Petrus Hispanus* (Berlin: Verlog der Akademie der Wissenschaften, 1937), p. 4.

[8] Louis Lachance, "Saint Thomas dans l'histoire de la logique," in *Etudes d'Histoire Littéraire et Doctrinale du XIIIe Siècle* (Paris: Vrin, 1932), p. 63.

Martin Grabmann, Bernhard Geyer,[9] Innocentius M. Bochenski,[10] the *Medieval Logic*[11] outline of the late Philotheus Boehner, and the present translator's own contribution[12] provide evidence of manuscript and incunabular investigations that rectify Prantl's presentation of mediaeval logic to such a point that new and just broad re-evaluations can now be achieved about the historical lines of scholastic logic.[13] Mention must be made here of a little known 1920 "Geschichte der Logik" which is integrated in a very informative *Lehrbuch der Logik* written by Theodore Ziehen.[14] Ziehen states quite properly that scholastic logic reached a peak after the thirteenth century.[15] However, it must be pointed out that such a statement does not entail the truth of this one: "After Ockham, the scholastics do not bring forth any important logicians."[16] In the history of ideas and systems, *importance* is not to be reduced to a subjective viewpoint or inclination, nor can it be confused with the present state of our knowledge. Any logician, any logical system, any logical distinction is of the greatest importance in itself. That the logician, the system, the distinction be known seems to be the only matter of importance. This remark applies to the most recent and monumental history of logic, namely: the *Formale Logik*[17] of I. M. Bochenski. In his review of that work, Fr. Ivo Thomas has described his confrere's weakness in these terms: ". . . little or no attention has been paid to the periods of development and breakdown at the opening and close respectively of the later Middle Ages."[18] The present translation of certain incunabular editions of these tracts of the *Logica Moderna* will, it is hoped, remedy such a lacuna, and help fill a gap in the history of Scholastic logic. Since the translated tracts were all originally appended to editions of Peter of Spain's *Summulae Logicales,* it is well to review briefly the influence of Peter and his *Summulae* in mediaeval logic.

[9] *Peter A b a e l a r d ' s philosophische Schriften* (Munster: Aschendorff, 1919-32).

[10] *Petri Hispani Summulae Logicales* ([Torino:] Domus Editorialis Marietti, S. Sedis Apostolicae et S. Rituum Typographi, 1947).

[11] *Medieval Logic, An Outline of its Development from 1250 to c. 1400* (Chicago: The University of Chicago Press, 1952).

[12] J. P. Mullally, *The Summulae Logicales of Peter of Spain* (Notre Dame, Ind.: Notre Dame University Press, 1945).

[13] In this respect, consult J. Ferrater Mora's study: "De Boecio a Alberto de Sajonia. Un fragmento de historia de la logica," in *Imago Mundi,* I (1954), 3-22.

[14] (Bonn: Marcus and Weber, 1920). The *erster Teil* covering the history of logic comprises 240 pp.

[15] *Op. cit.,* p. 72-73.

[16] *Ibid.,* p. 86.

[17] (Freiburg/München: Verlag Karl Alber, 1956). Now available in English: *A History of Formal Logic,* trans. and ed. by Ivo Thomas, (Notre Dame, Ind.: University of Notre Dame Press, 1961). We must note that the original bibliography (pp. 531-605) was simply photoreproduced (pp. 460-534).

[18] *The New Scholasticism,* XXXIII (1959), 393.

The author of the famous *Summulae* was born between 1210 and 1220 in Lisbon, Portugal. He was baptized Petrus Juliani. After completing his studies at the Cathedral school of his natal city, Peter registered at the University of Paris. The most ancient thirteenth century Parisian teacher of logic known to us is Jean Pagus whose philosophic career is situated around 1230. It must be noted that there are three extant logical tracts of Pagus: the *Appellationes*, the *Syncategoremata*, and the *Rationes super Predicamenta Aristotelis*. The English logician William of Shyreswood also taught at Paris before 1240. William wrote a small handbook of formal logic divided into six chapters: "de propositione," "de predicabili," "de syllogismo," "de locis dialecticis," "de proprietatibus terminorum," "de fallaciis." These tracts are entitled at times *Summulae Logicales*, or *Introductiones in Logicam*.[19] William also produced the *Syncategoremata*, and the opuscula: *Insolubilia, Obligationes*, and *Petitiones contrariorum*. At Paris, Peter Juliani studied logic under William, medicine and theology under Jean de Parme. It was during his stay at Paris that he acquired the "*cognomen* Petrus Hispanus (Peter of Spain) by which he has been made known to history."[20] Prior to 1245, Peter of Spain taught at Paris; in 1246, he was named professor of medicine at the University of Sienna. Between 1250 and 1276, Peter occupied various minor church positions. In 1272, Pope Gregory X summoned Peter to become his physician at Viterbo. In that capacity, Peter composed a *Thesaurus Pauperum* or medical text. His other writings included the *Summulae Logicales* whose authority and circulation soon became and remained extraordinary at the University of Paris and Oxford,[21] the *Tractatus maiorum fallaciorum*, and the *Syncategoremata*. Mention must also be made of Peter's *Liber de Anima*, a solid handbook of psychology, probably written in Italy after 1245.[22] Peter is also credited with commentaries on Aristotle, for example: *De Animalibus, De Morte et Vita, De Anima*, as well as with commentaries on the Pseudo-Dyonisius.[23]

Peter of Spain was elected Pope on September 8, 1276[24] and was

---

[19] Martin Grabmann, *Die Introductiones in logicam des Wilhelm von Shyreswood* (+ nach 1267), (München: Verlag der Bayerischen Akademie der Wissenschaften in Kommission bei der C. H. Beck'schen, 1937), 106 pp.

[20] Cf. Mullally, *op. cit.*, p. xviii.

[21] For a sampling of commentaries on Peter's *Summulae* by rival schools, cf., Etienne Gilson, *La philosophie au moyen-age* (3d ed.; Paris: Payot, 1947), p. 555.

[22] Fernand Van Steenberghen, "Le mouvement philosophique de 1200 à 1250," in *Le Mouvement Doctrinal du XIe au XIVe Siècle*, vol. 13 of the collection Histoire de l'Eglise, (Paris: Bloud & Gay, 1951), p. 199.

[23] One finds the bibliography of Peter of Spain in the *Histoire Littératre de la France*, tome XIX.

[24] Mullally, *op. cit.*, p. xx, indicates September 13. Van Steenberghen's date is accepted here, cf. *Les oeuvres et la doctrine de Siger de Brabant*

erroneously crowned as Pope John XXI rather than as Pope John XX, which he rightfully was. A few months later, on January 18, 1277, he issued a Papal Bull which commissioned Bishop Tempier of Paris to investigate errors which were then being taught at the University of Paris. On March 7, 1277 Bishop Tempier issued his famous condemnation of two hundred and nineteen propositions which were being propagated at Paris.

Although Bishop Tempier exceeded the powers granted to him by the Papal commission, the condemnation by the Bishop can be regarded as being subsequently approved by the Pope because a Papal Bull of April 28, 1277 ordered Bishop Tempier to effect a purification of the errors being taught at Paris. The end of Peter's Pontificate came unexpectedly when he died on May 20, 1277 from injuries sustained a few days before when the roof of a private apartment in the Papal palace at Viterbo collapsed on him.

The body of logical writings of Peter of Spain divides itself into two main parts. The first part comprises an intelligent abridgment of the *Organon*, making up the *Summulae Logicales*. The second part embraces certain opuscula under the title *Parva Logicalia*. One of Prantl's most serious blunders relates to the antecedents and authenticity of the *Summulae Logicales*. Indeed, Prantl regarded the *Summulae* as a translation into latin of a Greek manual of logic written by Michael Psellos. Bernhard Geyer and Martin Grabmann have established that, in fact, the relationship was reversed.[25] Since then, the present translator has shown, on the basis of contemporaneous evidence, that Petrus Hispanus is the author of the *Summulae*.[26] Hence, it is held now that the tradition or filiation of the *Summulae* is latin, and that it comprises within 1200 and 1250 three great masters: William of Shyreswood, Petrus himself, and Lambert of Auxerre. Martin Grabmann has made a comparison of the texts of these three mediaeval logicians, and, contrary to common opinion, he has taken the position that Lambert has relied on Petrus rather than the reverse.[27] For his part, Geyer has produced evidence tending to establish 1253 as the latest possible date for the composition of Lambert's *Summulae*, this being years later than the probable date of Petrus' writing.[28]

(Bruxelles: Palais des Académies, 1938), p. 53.

[25] Grabmann, *Bearbeitungen*, p. 14: "The textbook with which Psellus is credited is rather a translation of the *Summulae Logicales* of Peter of Spain."

[26] Mullally, *op. cit.*, p. xv.

[27] "Handschriftliche Forschungen und Funde zu den philosophischen des Petrus Hispanus. . . ." in *Sitzungs-*

berichte der Bayerischen Akademie der Wissenschaften, Philosophisch-historischen Klasse, IX (1936), p. 42.

[28] "Zu den *Summulae Logicales* des Petrus Hispanus und Lambert von Auxerre," in *Philosophisches Jahrbuch*, v. 50, Fulda, 1937, p. 512. Lambert's *Summulae* are as yet unedited.

[4]

From the middle of the twelfth century to the middle of the fifteenth century a progressive distinction came to establish itself between the *logica antiqua* and the *logica moderna*. The *University Records and Life in the Middle Ages* of the great historian Lynn Thorndike make it possible for us to realize this progressive movement within the history of logic by comparing two university records. The first one consists of a statute of the University of Paris concerning students of the English nation who were candidates for the licentiate in arts in 1252:

> Moreover, a bachelor coming up for the licentiate in arts at Paris should be twenty years old or at least in his twentieth year, and of honorable life and laudable conversation. . . . Also before he is admitted to examination he shall give personal security . . . that he has attended lectures in arts for five years or four at least . . . that he has heard the books of Aristotle on the Old Logic, namely, the *Praedicamenta* and *Periarmeniae* at least twice in ordinary lectures and once cursorily, the *Six Principles* at least once in ordinary lectures and once cursorily, the three first books of the *Topics* and the *Divisions* once in ordinary lectures or at least cursorily, the *Topics* of Aristotle and *Elenci* . . . the *Prior Analytics* . . . the *Posterior Analytics*. . . . Also that he shall have heard *Priscian minor* (books 17-18) . . ., *Priscian major* (books 1-16). . . .[29]

The second document is a folio analysis of a manuscript of 200 leaves containing the "texts required for A.B. Degree at Erfurt, 1420":

> Fols. 1-17: Of the shorter edition of Donatus
> fols. 17-28: also the second part of the *Doctrinale* of Alexander of Villa Dei
> fols. 28-41: also the Supposition of Terms of Thomas Maulivelt
> fols. 47-47: also the treatise of Confusions and *Sinkathegreumata* of the same
> fols. 48-51: also his treatise of Ampliations
> fols. 51-52: also his treatise of Restrictions
> fols. 52-55: also his treatise of Appellations
> fol. 55: also his treatise of Alienations
>   also his treatise of Remotions
> fols. 55-64: also his treatise of Consequences, otherwise that of John Sutton of England . . .
> fols. 64-79: also the treatise of Richard Biligam On the Proofs of Propositions . . .
> fols. 79-82: also the treatise of Obligations of Hollandrinus . . .
> fols. 82-83: also the treatise of Insolubles of the same Hollandrinus . . .
> fols. 83-98: also of the *Isagoge* of Porphyry
> fols. 98-114: also of the *Predicamenta* of Aristotle

[29] (New York: Columbia University Press, 1944), pp. 53-54, record n. 26.

fols. 114-122; also of the *Peryermenia of Aristotle*
fols. 122-141: also of the books of *Piror Analytics* of Aristotle
fols. 141-154: also of the books of *Posterior Analytics* of Aristotle
fols. 154-162: also of the books of *Elenci* of Aristotle
fols. 162-187: also of the books of *Physics* of Aristotle
fols. 187-198: also of the books *Of the Soul* of Aristotle. . . .[30]

In this movement from the Old Logic to Modern Logic, the first six tracts of Peter's *Summulae* represent a thorough practical analysis of the *logica antiqua* with one very important omission. Nowhere, as far as we know, does Peter of Spain treat of the *Posterior Analytics* of Aristotle. The seventh tract of the *Summulae* is known variously as the tract *de proprietatibus terminorum*, the *parva logicalia*, or the *logica moderna*. This seventh tract deals with "supposition," "relatives," "amplification," "appellation," "restriction," "distribution," and "exponibles." However, the name *logica moderna* extends to the four additional tracts: *Syncategorematics, Obligations, Insolubles,* and *Consequences*. In contrast to the strict Aristotelian mediaeval logic, the *parva logicalia* or *logica moderna* emphasizes the *new* or *modern* elements of logic, or represents the inception of modern logic. One may recall that Philotheus Boehner has already presented us with a text of the late *Middle Ages* which explains the designation of certain treatises of modern logic by the title of *Parva Logicalia*. Specifically, the unknown author of the text relates ancient logic to *modern* mediaeval logic as follows:

> (1) They are treated in small books and presented in the form of tracts, whilst the works of Aristotle are offered in the style of "principal" books. (2) Only the principles of these tracts are laid down by Aristotle. Now, the principles, though few and concise, wield tremendous power. In relation, then, to the principles the tracts are called "small," that is, they are viewed as comparatively insignificant and of less moment. (3) They are concerned with rudimentary elements, viz., with terms and their properties, which are the ultimate parts of the subject matter of logic. (4) These tracts are "small" by comparison with other works *composed by Peter of Spain*.[31] (italics ours)

It is acknowledged that the contents of these tracts were tentatively formulated or regulated by Aristotle and the Stoics. However, the descriptive or metalogical advance belongs to the thirteenth, fourteenth, and fifteenth centuries. The field of these tracts is a very rich and interesting one in itself, as well as in its applications in the context of mediaeval educational methodology or of the history of mediaeval science.[32] One surely cannot agree with Professor Vignaux's remarks to the effect that:

[30] *Ibid.*, pp. 296-97, record n. 119.
[31] *Ibid.*, p. 117.

[32] One is happy to note that research has already been extended to the

[6]

This *logica modernorum* is a systematic treatise of the properties of terms, that one finds in the Englishman William Shyreswood, in the Dominican Lambert of Auxerre, and in a manual running through the fourteenth and fifteenth centuries; the *Summulae Logicales* of a certain Petrus Hispanus, traditionally identified with Pope John XXI. Unhappily, these authors are for us no more than names: since Prantl, in the last century, no researcher has been tempted by the tedious work of dressing up the inventory of their achievements.[33] (translation ours)

Besides revealing the intrinsic worth of the tracts themselves, the present translations make it possible for students, teachers, historians of philosophy, and historians of logic to better appreciate the continuity of *Formal Logic* and the progress of mediaeval logic over ancient logic. The originality of these treatises and their observable force from the thirteenth through the fifteenth century are thus transferred into the twentieth century. An examination of the source and contents of the translated tracts is in order.

ANALYSIS OF THE TRACTS

In his earlier work, the translator had compiled a very useful, if not complete, list of incunabular editions of the *Summulae* of Peter of Spain.[34] Without doubt, the list can be used to signify the virtue and influence of the *Summulae*. This partial numbered inventory of the extant editions is as follows: (a) without commentary, nn. 1-51; (b) with anonymous commentaries, nn. 52-53; (c) with commentaries of the Cologne Thomists, nn. 54-77; (d) with Arnoldus de Tungris' commentary, nn. 78-79; with Joannes Eckius' commentary, n. 80; with Georgius Bruxellensis' commentary, nn. 8-105b; with Gerardus de Harderwijck's commentary, nn. 106-10; with Gerardus Listrius' commentary, nn. 111-12; with Johannes de Monte's commentary, nn. 120-21; with Nicholas de Orbellis' commentary, nn. 122-24c; with Conradus Pschlacher's commentary, nn. 125-26; with Eelco Schagius' commentary, n. 127; with Petrus Tartaretus' commentary, nn. 128-40; with Nicholas Tinctor's commentary, n. 141; with Johannes Versor's commentary, nn. 142-66. It is noteworthy that these commentators represent just as many areas of blank spots in the complex history of logical movements and schemas, and that this compilation is incomplete.

The tracts offered in translation here have been collated from two incunabular editions of Peter's *Summulae*. One edition is dated 1489,

Regule Solvendi Sophismata of William Heytesbury and their influence in Mathematical Physics, cf. Curtis Wilson, *William Heytesbury: Medieval Logic and the Rise of Mathematical Physics*, (Madison: The University of Wisconsin Press, 1956).
[33] *La pensée au moyen age* (Paris: Colin, 1948), pp. 63-64.
[34] *Ibid.*, pp. 133-58.

and listed as n. 8702 in Ludwig Hain's *Repertorium Bibliographicum.* Hain's description is as follows (translation ours):

> Conjuncts of all the Tracts of Peter of Spain. Also the *syncategoremata* and the *parva logicalia* with the text according to the doctrine of the eloquent Thomas Aquinas according to the process of the masters of Cologne teaching in the bursa Montis. F 2 a: In respect to the beginning of the summulae (sic) of Peter of Spain, etc. At the end: Conjuncts of the six tracts of Peter of Spain according to the doctrine of St. Thomas Aquinas, diligently collected by the zeal of the masters of Cologne teaching in the bursa Montis, and recently skillfully printed for the practice of the neophytes in logic. In the year of the Lord, 1489. They finished happily. Then F 1 a: the tract on supposition of P.H. begins: in respect to the beginning of the *parva logicalia*, etc. . . . F 74 a: The text with conjuncts of all the tracts of the *parva logicalia* of Peter of Spain is finished. Also the text of the same concerning the *syncategoremata* which some call the eighth tract, together with some others, according to the process of the masters of Cologne teaching in the bursa of Master Lambertus de Monte, distinguished professor of arts and sacred theology, corrected again and again with the most laborious study, and now finally printed. In the year fourteen eighty nine, on the day before the ninth of December. (Cologne: Henr. Quentell, 1489).

The second edition is from 1494, and is n. 8705 in Hain's catalogue. Its description is (translation ours):

> Text and conjuncts of all the tracts of Peter of Spain, also of the *parva logicalia* and the tract of the *syncategoremata* which some call the eighth (tract), together with some astutely added, corrected again and again most diligently according to the indestructible doctrine of the eloquent Thomas Aquinas, and according to the frequent exercise of the masters of Cologne collected in this one book. F 2 a: in respect to the beginning of the summulae of Peter of Spain according to the doctrine of St. Thomas Aquinas, diligently collected by the zeal of the masters of Cologne teaching in the bursa Montis, and recently skillfully printed for the practice of the neophytes in logic. In the year of the Lord, 1494, fifteenth of June. They finished happily. A table which explains begins on the same page. F 275 b: the table of questions is finished. Add. F 1 a tit: Conjuncts over and above all the tracts of the *parva logicalia* of Peter of Spain, and over and above the three tracts of the text of the *moderni* most beautifully annotated in the case of arguments and expositions again corrected most diligently according to the inviolable process of the masters of Cologne teaching in the bursa Montis. F 2 a: in respect to the beginning of the *parva logicalia*, ignorance of which, etc. . . . F 120 a: Tract of the parva logicalia follows the tract of the *syncategoremata*. F 148 a: And these statements regarding the syncategoremata suffice. (Cologne: no printer?, 1494).

These descriptions clearly indicate that these editions belong to the group of the Cologne Thomists, and that they had an elementary purpose. The conjuncts mentioned in these notations refer to the *Syncategorematics,* the *Obligations,* the *Insolubles,* and the *Consequences.*

The task of removing linguistic obstacles to the attainment of truth and to the correct communication of thought has been consistently and necessarily recognized in the history of the development of classical and traditional logical theory, including among others as proponents, Aristotle, Cicero, Augustine, Abelard, and Peter of Spain. The analysis of syncategorematic words[35] by which "truth or falsity is caused in a proposition" is found in the seventh treatise of Tract VI of Peter's *Summulae,* the *Exponibilia,* and is in keeping with this tradition, being motivated by it and developed within it. The sources of the *Exponibilia* themselves are to be found in the Old Logic, as in Aristotle's treatment of "beginning" and "ending,"[36] or his treatment of "infinite" in the *Physics;*[37] in Abelard's analysis of the consignificative functioning of "alone," an exclusive syncategorematic word,[38] or his treatment of comparison in his discussion of the categories,[39] which treatment is based on Priscian;[40] or in Priscian's own treatment of superlatives.[41] I. M. Bochenski has doubted Peter's authorship of the *Exponibilia,* but recent research seems to invalidate such a position.[42]

The *Syncategorematics* play a vital role in the development of mediaeval logic. On their intrinsic importance, Philotheus Boehner once remarked: "It is these formal elements which enable us to make inferences, and for that reason they are the main subject of logic."[43] Surely, as a tract, it represents a summing up of previus progress, and a jumping off place for new developments. It is a more extensive and scientific analysis of the generic and specific features of syncategorematic expressions than is found in the *Exponibilia.* It treats of not only all the words mentioned in the *Exponibilia* but also of many additional ones not covered before. The analysis is combined with a proliferation of rules arising from the various logical compositions into which a

35 For the origin of the term "syncategoremata" in the history of logic, cf. Ziehen, *op. cit.,* p. 584, and J. R. O'Donnell, "The *Syncategoremata* of William of Sherwood," in *Medieval Studies,* III (1941), 47.

36 Aristotle, *Metaphysics* v. 1 and 17.

37 Aristotle, *Physics* iv. 11. 219ᵃ 22-23; 219ᵇ 11; esp. iii. 4. 209ᵃ 1-8.

38 *Peter Abaelard, Logica Ingredientibus,* ed. by Bernhard Geyer in the *Beitrage Zur Geschichte* . . ., XXI (Münster: Aschendorff, 1933),

Glossa super Periermeneias, p. 483.

39 *Ibid., Glossa super Praedicamenta* . . ., pp. 160, 200, 209, 233, 243-48.

40 *Institutiones Grammaticae,* ed. by Martin Hertz (Leipzig: Teubner, 1855-59, III, I, 8, 13.

41 *Ibid.*

42 *Petri Hispani* . . ., p. xiv, against Mullally, *op. cit.,* pp. 104ff., and Wilson, *op cit.,* p. 171, n. 19.

43 *O c k h a m, Philosophical Writings* (London: Nelson, 1957), p. xxxi.

syncategorematic word can enter. Furthermore, whereas the *Exponibilia* merely states a few rules and a few examples, the *Syncategoremata* contains over fifty sophisms illustrative of the uses of syncategorematic expressions, and requires a knowledge or understanding of the contents of the treatises on the properties of terms as well as of the logical, physical, and metaphysical principles of Aristotle, Boethius, Porphyry, and of the grammatical principles of Priscian and Donatus. According to the *Exponibilia,* an exponible proposition is simply one which is obscure due to a syncategorematic word. The *Syncategoremata* sets forth in detail what specifically differentiates the consignification of each of the syncategorematics in affirmative and negative contexts, and in their functioning in various adjunctions with transcendental and categorical generic conceptions. Although the syncategorematic units of propositions, viz., adverbs, prepositions, conjunctions, etc., lack signification as such, they are not meaningless. Indeed, they turn out to be the most meaningful or the most determining logical elements in propositions. Propositions containing such words are resolvable into composite statements which clearly express or reveal the obscurity and confusion of the original statements. The *Syncategorematics* amply demonstrate this and in so doing reveals itself as a natural and *formal* extension of not only the *Exponibles* but of the other treatises of the *De Proprietatibus Terminorum* as well. In connection with the sophisms of the *Syncategorematics,* and other translated tracts, it should be noted that they are not sophisms in the Aristotelian sense of fallacious arguments. Rather, they are, as Gaston Wallerand has already explained,[44] scholarly exercises, or concrete examples used to practice the rules of logic made known to the students. The sophisms fulfill a double function: (a) they illustrate the consignificative nature of syncategorematic expressions, and (b) they train the students in the detection of invalid arguments or the demonstration of the truth or falsity of a proposition taken as a basis of discussion. The usual procedure of the sophisms in the *Syncategorematics* is *first* to state a proposition with a syncategorematic word, *second* to set up a proof which is followed by a disproof, *third* to solve the problem. Virtually, at the end of the tract, there is a presentation of the various modes of solution in general.[45] This integral part of the exercises of the mediaeval schools came to constitute the major part of logical works. Again, we see the *Syncategorematics* representing not only a summation of earlier logical theory but also a point of departure for subsequent logical evolution. In other words,

---

[44] *Les oeuvres de Siger de Courtrai* in Les Philosophes Belges, VIII, (Louvain: Éditions de L'Institut Supérieur de Philosophie, 1913), pp. 27ff.

[45] Cf below, p. 112.

the utilization of sophisms reached such proportions that eventually such authors as Albert of Saxony, Heytesbury, and Buridan compiled sophisms into tracts entitled *Sophismata*.

The *Obligations* and *Insolubles* are developments of a basic principle drawn from Aristotle's *Prior Analytics*[46] and *Metaphysics*.[47] Common aims unite these two tracts, to discuss the art which enables tyro logicians to escape from logical traps, and to entrap the logically unskilled. Necessary to an art are the definitions of technical terms, fixed rules of action, and productions that agree with the rules. These three factors provide the delineation of the *Obligations*, for the tract states first the descriptions of such fundamental terms as "obligation," "obligate," "the relevant"; it then offers seven rules to be practiced, and finally it gives examples involving applied rules. In the abstract, an obligation is a concession of the possible that prevents the admission of the impossible. In the concrete, the obligation refers to the debating arts, or the functions of debaters in controversies. The dozen examples in the tract amply illustrate this point. Since Peter's *Summulae* was produced to provide a compendium of practical rules for neophytes in logic within a setting of university dialectics, it stands to reason that such a tract be appended to the *Summulae* to form part of the training of students within the university life, logic being propaedeutic to the study of philosophy and theology.

The tract on Insolubles is also constructed around three points: what propositions can be called insoluble, what causes insolubility in propositions, and examples illustrative of insolubility. By "insolubles"[48] are meant paradoxical difficulties or propositions that offer intrinsic difficulties to the discernment of their truth or falsity. The *principle* of the difficulty is that "from what is so follows what is not so." A secondary signification comes to reflect on the direct signification, either immediately as in the case of "Sortes is saying what is false," or mediately as in the case when Sortes says: "Plato speaks the truth," while Plato maintains on the contrary that: "Sortes is saying what is false." The intrinsic value of the insolubles cannot be underestimated anymore since their rediscovery created a crisis in the foundations of mathematics which, in some measure, led to the rich developments of mathematical logic, the intuitionism of Brouwer, and the axiomatics of Hilbert. Unlike the *Obligations*, the bibliography on the *Insolubles* is quite extensive. It suffices to single out Kurt Grelling's study, "The Logical Paradoxes," in *Mind*, XLV (1936), and

---

[46] *Prior Analytics* i. 13. 32ª 18-20.
[47] *Metaphysics* ix. 4. 1047ᵇ 18-19.

[48] For the origin of the term "insolubilia" in the history of logic, cf. Wallerand, *op. cit.*, p. 27ff.

Alexander Koyre's, "The Liar," in *Philosophy and Phenomenological Research*, VI (1946).[49]

The closing tract deals with *Consequences*. A "consequence" is a composite or compound statement denoting that one statement in this composition is a sequel of the other. Since the *Consequences* best exemplify the nature of logic as the science of permissible inferences, and since logical techniques help greatly in recognizing the structure and contents of philosophical texts—*a fortiori* of logic texts—let us present in conclusion a commentary on the Consequences in Modern Dress.

CONSEQUENCES IN MODERN DRESS

The notation will be borrowed from the excellent work of P. Suppes, *Introduction to Logic*.[50] Departures from this notation will be clearly indicated. The expressions "consequence" and "consequent" in the translation will mean "implication" and "conclusion" in the symbolic transcriptions and the commentary. References to the translated test will read as follows: (141) 6-8 to mean page 141, line 6 to 8.

   I. *Definition of Implication*

     (141)   6-8 $p{\rightarrow}q$ is a valid implication.
               8-10 $(p{\rightarrow}\text{-}q)$ & $q{\rightarrow}p$
              10-16 The text notes carefully that the connective is to be understood inferentially and not materially. This notation is important since it stipulates negation as possible only for the subject and predicate terms. It excludes the possibility of negative implication.

   II. *Definition of Antecedent, p*

     (141)   20-22

   III. *Definition of Consequent, q*

     (141)   23-24

   IV. *Definition of Inferential Sign*

     (141)   25-27 The inferential sign denotes a sequence of terms in an implication.

   V. *Law of Simplification*

     (141)   28-36 $(p\ \&\ q){\rightarrow}p$ is valid. This corresponds to the law of simplification. The expression "consequence" in the text refers to "p&q." It could be called a compound subject to distinguish it from an implication. A substantive constant

---

[49] One could also consult C. I. Lewis and C. H. Langford, *Symbolic Logic* (New York: The Century Co., 1932), pp. 438ff.

[50] (Princeton: Van Nostrand, 1957).

could be used in certain contexts, e.g. $(\exists e)$ $(Pe \& Qe)$.

The following example is used to indicate an invalid implication: $(p \& q) \to (p \to q)$, indicating that the implication must be denied. There is thus a recognition that implication can be denied, or that there is no implication.

In the example: $(p \to q) \& -(P \& Q)$, the text comes close to stating the law of negation for implication. The text is short of the law, because the concept of tautological equivalence is lacking, and the understanding of negative implication is not clear.

VI. *Demonstration of Valid Implication*

(141) 37-39 $(p \to q \ \& \ p) \to q$
$(p, \to q, \ \& \ p,) \to q,$
Demonstration that the validity of an implication depends on its formal structure, and is valid for variables with the same signification. Even if primitive, this recognition of the necessity for similarity of signification in substituting variables anticipates the modern development of class and member concepts to satisfy this condition.

VII. *Confusion of Meaning* and *Form of Proposition*

(142) 3-5   The text claims the following to be insufficient
       10-25   to establish validity: $[(p \to q) \& -(-p)] \to q$. The symbolic translation of this implication clearly shows its validity. The text confuses meaning and form of proposition. In modern symbolism, "$-(-p) \longleftrightarrow p$" is an accepted reality.
       17-25   The text asserts the validity of
$$[(p \to q \ \& \ p) \ \& \ (p \to q \ \& \ q)] \to p \to q.$$
The usefulness of this inference could be questioned.

VIII. *Absolute and Ut Nunc Validity*

(142) 26-40 The distinction dealt with in this text is not an invalid one, as it is claimed. In fact, it is not a question of the division of validity, but rather of the change of signification of terms which is not always easily expressed in language. Hence, it would seem that
$$(x) \ (Mx \to Ax) \quad \to (\exists x) \quad (Mx \to Ax)$$
is valid, while
$$(x) \ (Mx \to Ax) \quad \to (\exists x,) \quad (Mx, \to Ax,)$$
is not an implication or is not valid.

$\begin{pmatrix}142\\143\end{pmatrix}$ 41-43   The passage seems to suggest that in certain
        1-15   cases, implications of the form
$$(p \to q \ \& \ p) \to q$$

[13]

might now be valid, whereas they might previously have been invalid depending upon the truth of the implication in regard to temporal circumstances. Thus, the division of validity into (a) as of now, and (b) absolutely. Modern logic would submit that temporal considerations are extralogical, and arise only when an attempt is made to interpret the terms of the logical model factually. Factual elements, such as temporal factors, should not apply to specific logical formulations. That is not to say that logical models cannot be derived to cope with such temporal factors. This is a sensitive area which has been treated in a most serious and sensible way, in reference to E. A. Moody's interpretation of Ockham's Consequences, by J. D. Beierle in a Ph.D. dissertation (Philadelphia: University of Pennsylvania, 1957), (esp. pp. 101-108), entitled *Ockham's Theory of Consequences.*

IX. *Definition of Formal Implication*

(143) 17 ff. Formal implication is defined as:
(144) 1-22

$$(p \rightarrow q) \,\&\, (q \rightarrow r) \rightarrow (p \rightarrow r)$$

given a constant signification of terms and of logical connectives throughout. Difficulties of material implication are avoided if one realizes that the correct symbolization of the example given should read:

$$[(x) \ (Mx \rightarrow Ax) \,\&\, (x,) \ Sx, \rightarrow Ax,)] \rightarrow (x)(x,) \ (Mx \rightarrow Sx,)$$

The language may seem to indicate identical signification, while symbolization reveals why this apparent *non-sequitur* has no conclusion. Material implication can be considered valid only if the interpreted data conforms to the logical model and not to the linguistic model. The latter is inadequate on many counts. In this instance, it is ambiguous.

The text also indicates the method of *reductio ad absurdum* as follows:

$$[p \rightarrow q \,\&\, -(p \,\&\, -p)] \rightarrow q$$

The example of the derivation of valid conclusions from the convertible to the convertible may be symbolized in this way:

$$(x) \ [(Mx \rightarrow Rx) \,\&\, (Mx \longleftrightarrow Ux)] \rightarrow (\exists x)(Ux \rightarrow Rx).$$

X. *Some Rules of Consequences*

1. (144) 23-27 The valid implication:
       28-43

$$-q \,\&\, (p \rightarrow q) \rightarrow -p$$

is the equivalent of the tautology, *Modus*

Tollendo Tollens. This is proved from the law of absurdity:

$$(p{\rightarrow}q \,\&\, {-}q){\rightarrow}{-}p$$

The fallacy of the denial of the antecedent is also stated as invalid:

$$(p{\rightarrow}q \,\&{-}p){\rightarrow}{-}q.$$

2. (145) 8-19 The text gives as valid:

$$(p{\rightarrow}q \,\&\, p){\rightarrow}q$$

This corresponds to the law of detachment.

The text gives as invalid:

$$(p{\rightarrow}q \,\&\, {-}p){\rightarrow}\text{-}q$$

This corresponds to the fallacy of denying the antecedent.

The text gives as invalid:

$$(p{\rightarrow}q \,\&\, q){\rightarrow}p$$

It corresponds to the fallacy of affirming the consequent.

3. (146) 33 ff. $(x)\,(\exists y)\,[(Ay{\rightarrow}Ax) \,\&\, {-}(Ax{\rightarrow}Ay)]$
(147)-(150) The discussion of the rule would be greatly simplified by symbolization, thus showing that the examples do not conform to the logical model.

4. (150) 35 ff. $(\exists x)\,(Mx \,\&\, {-}Rx){\rightarrow}(\exists y)\,(Ay \,\&\, {-}Ry)$
(151) 1-13 is affirmed as valid. Symbolically, it cannot stand as valid. The second example is declared invalid on account of extralogical elements concerning temporal factors. In fact, it is invalid because it conforms to a logical model which, as stated, is itself invalid. For the same reason, the third example is also invalid. It differs from the model in that it has a compound subject. The fourth example is cited as invalid, and the text recognizes the value of exclusiveness.

5. (151) 14-18 The text holds as valid:

$$(\exists x)\,(Sx \,\&\, Mx_0{\rightarrow}Ax_0) \quad {}_0{=}\text{only}$$

This axiom would be valid if the concept of the term Mx_0 was included in the concept of the term Ax_0. Since the argument is stated to be from an inferior to a superior, this understanding is implicit.

6. (151) 19-33 Implication from distributed superior to inferior. The considerations given by the text concerning "beginning" and "ceasing" do not apply.

[15]

7. (152) 30-32 (x) $(Mx{\to}Ax) {\to} (\exists x) (Ax{\to}Mx)$

8. (153) 29-43 (x) $(Mx{\to}Rx) {\to} (x) (-Rx {\to} -Mx)$
                      (x) $(Sx{\to}-Rx) {\to} (x) (Rx{\to}-Sx)$

9. (154) 1-8 (x) $(Rx{\to}Mx){\to} (\exists x) (Mx{\to}Rx)$
                     (x) $(-Rx{\to}Mx){\to} (\exists x) (Mx{\to}-Rx)$

10. (156) 26-32 Both are valid:

$$p \vee q \& -p {\to} q$$
$$p \vee q \& -q {\to} p$$

11. (156) 33-37 $(p{\to}q) \& p {\to} q$ is valid.

12. (156) 38-42 $(p{\to}q) \& -q {\to} -p$ is valid.

The authors hold with Philotheus Boehner that in "the theory of consequences we . . . discover some of the finest achievements of scholastic logic."[51] Rules of consequence were known to scholastic logicians and theologians in the thirteenth century. As Boehner stated, the theory itself grew out of systematic development of the contents of the *Topics* of Aristotle,[52] which had started to exert tremendous influence in the Occident even during the twelfth century. The topical rules had been set forth enthymematically by Aristotle, a.v., they required a third proposition to become syllogisms, a fact which led the scholastic logicians to divide consequences into those which required a third proposition and those which did not. This fact coupled with the fact that the nonenthymemic consequences treated are concerned with or equivalent to Aristotle's *Topics* led Boehner to assert that it is reasonable to assume that "the topical rules are the historical starting points of the consequential rules."[53]

The study of the history of logic as relevant to this and to the other tracts which have been translated serves to confirm anew the view that "The historical continuity in the development of human thought is such that the entire succession of men may be regarded as if only one man has always existed and is continually learning."[54] For from the vantage point of the Tracts of the Logica Moderna one can indeed look backward but also forward.[55]

[51] *Op. cit.*, p. 52.
[52] *Ibid.*
[53] *Ibid.*, p. 53.
[54] Mullally, *op. cit.*, p. xxxviii.
[55] The recent and important monograph of Lucien Martinelli, *Thomas D'-Aquin et L'Analyse Linguistique* (Conférence Albert- le- Grand 1963. Montréal: Institut d'Etudes Médiévales et Paris: Vrin), suggests the possibility of delimiting, within the *logica nova* and *moderna*, a better model of really *scholastic* logical analysis based on the history and doctrine of the *De Modis Significandi*, in which "les options logiques sont tributaires des options épistémologiques." (pp. 52 and 66-71).

Treatise on Syncategorematic Words

Because a thing is or is not, a proposition is said to be true or false. But truth or falsity is caused in a proposition by syncategorematic words, such as "only," "alone," "but," "with the exception of," and so on. Therefore syncategorematic words signify something or other. But they do not signify things capable of functioning as subjects or predicates. Therefore they signify characteristics of things which are characteristics of things capable of functioning as subjects or predicates. However, there is nothing in a true or false statement except a subject and a predicate and their characteristics. Nevertheless they do not signify characteristics of that which is a subject or of that which is a predicate, as "white," "black," "well," "badly," and the like, do; rather they signify a characteristic of a subject as subject or of a predicate as predicate. And *"syncategorema"* is composed of *"σύν,"* that is, *"with"* and *"κατηγόρημα,"* that is, *"subject"* or *"predicate,"* as it were consignificative. These must be discussed in this treatise and primarily the former.

Since such characteristics constitute a difficulty in propositions on account of the nature of the negation which is understood in them—as will become evident through their exposition—negation must be discussed first as a consequence. But because according to Aristotle,[1] affirmation is understood in every negation, since negation does not possess the quality of being known except through affirmation nor privation except through a quality (*habitus*), we now discuss affirmation and negation and multiple composition. Whence to understand negation fully, one must first consider affirmation. Because affirmation consists of affirmative composition, and because negation, its opposite, is diversified in accordance with a diversity of composition, on that account we must first consider composition.

Composition is the union of possible components resulting from a proportion of act and potency: for every composition requires act and potency, and along with this a union of these to each other which is caused by the tendency of act toward potency. Compositions, however, are real or logical. A real composition is one whose extremes are distinct from each other. This composition is of four kinds: one kind is the composition of integral parts; another type is that of essential parts; another kind is that of capacities, as the composition of the capacities of the soul in relation to one another or with the soul [itself]; another is that of an accident with a subject, as of whiteness with the wall of a house. A logical composition is one whose extremes are dis-

---

[1] *Metaphysicae*, iv. 2. 1004ª 10-16.

tinguished by reason alone, whether they are real or not, as is the composition of a quality with a substance in a noun or of a genus and a differentia in a species. As regards logical composition, some are signified in a word; others, however, in a proposition. Certainly that which belongs to a word is a composition of the essential and accidental modes of signifying (*modorum significandi*) of the eight parts of speech, to treat of which at length belongs to the grammarian. In relation to what has been proposed we discuss only the composition of the modes of signifying of a noun, a verb, and a participle, through whose negation an infinite term can come into existence, and the composition of a perfect proposition through whose negation a negative proposition comes into existence.

Now in the case of a noun there is a composition of a quality with a substance, because a noun is said to signify a substance with a quality. One ought not to understand that it signifies a true substance, because then there would be no nouns of accidents. Neither should it be understood that a noun signifies according to a mode of substance, i.e., of subsistence (*per se stare*), because then adjectives would not be nouns. Rather it is understood that it signifies according to a mode of substance, i.e., a mode of permanence, which belongs both to substantives and to adjectives. Nor should it be understood that it signifies a true quality, because then there would not be nouns for substances and nonentities. Rather it signifies according to the mode of a quality or according to the mode of a determinant. Therefore such composition is not a characteristic of things but of the modes of signifying.

If one objects that, since quality and substance are different and every word signifying different things is equivocal, therefore a noun, because it signifies a substance with a quality, will be equivocal, which is inadmissable, therefore in a noun there is not a composition of a quality with a substance, the response is that there are four modes in which different things happen to be signified equally by the same word. In the first mode, whenever different things are signified equally by the same word, as in the case of the noun "dog" (*canis*).[2] In the second mode, whenever different things are signified according to the prior and the posterior as in the noun "healthy" or "being." In the third mode, whenever any noun signifies one thing by a proper imposition and the rest by transference (*transsumptione*), as is clear in the case of the verb "to laugh" (*ridere*). These three modes rightly produce equivocation. In the fourth mode, different things are signified by the same word whenever one is the basis for understanding the

2 "*Canis*" denotes "*a dog*" and "*a star.*"

other or the principle for understanding the other, as form is the basis for understanding that which is the form. And thus a quality is signified as a signifying principle; but a substance is signified by a noun as that which is signified or understood by the quality itself. And because one is understood through the other, it follows in this case that there are not different significations but only one. On this account, this mode of signifying many things does not produce equivocation, just as when I see a color and an object colored throughout its magnitude, they are not different sights but only one, because color is the reason for seeing the magnitude in which it is.

Therefore one must note that the composition of a noun is twofold. One is the composition of an essential quality with a substance, as in the case of a substantive noun, as "man" has for its object the reality under humanity. There the reality is a substance and humanity is a quality of it. The other is the composition of an accidental quality with a substance, as exists in the case of adjectival nouns; for example, "white" signifies an accident in relation to an indefinite substance which is contained in such a noun as a substance and the accident as a quality. And in each composition of a quality with a substance, the quality is compounded with a substance without an intermediate because of a tendency which it has toward the substance, as every form and every accident are naturally united in that in which they are. For if such a composition be other than and distinct from the quality and from the substance, it would be united with them, and, therefore, without an intermediate. And then for the same reason it will have to be determined in the first way or through an intermediate. However, one should ask about that intermediate through which it would be united with the extremes. The process then would be infinite unless something were naturally united with another.

In a verb, however, there is a composition of an act with an intrinsic substance, as for example, "He is running" *(currit)* signifies a thing combined with the act of running; and the thing is regarded as a substance and the running as an act. The reason for this is that although a verb signifies an act concretely, it necessarily implies an indefinite substance. This is the substance united in the verb. But that substance does not function as a subject in the proposition. Rather it is predicated in the proposition, as when one says: "Sortes is running," running is not predicated absolutely and abstractly but rather the reality is predicated under the aspect of running; just as it is clear that in saying: "Sortes is white," the sense is not "Sortes is whiteness," rather it means: "Sortes is a thing having whiteness." This intrinsic composition of the verb is the union of an act implied by the verb with an intrinsic substance.

[19]

Similarly in the case of a participle there is a composition of a united act with a united substance, as for example, "reading" only signifies the same as "who reads." Whence "who" affirms substance; it affirms indefinite substance and "reads" affirms a determinate act. From this it is clear that a verb and a participle do not differ so far as the signified is concerned because each signifies an act conjoined with an intrinsic substance. Therefore Priscian[3] says that a participle has reference to that which is signified by a verb under the accidents of a noun. However, verb and participle differ in the mode of signifying. A verb signifies an act or movement in the manner of going out of a substance in the case of action or in the manner of going into a substance in the case of passion, by virtue of which it signifies in a mode predicable of another and it implies an act in a mode of being distinct from an exterior substance and for this reason it implies the composition which belongs to a proposition. A participle signifies an act in a mode of implying a substance or in a mode of an act conjoined with a united substance, but not in the sense of going into a substance or of going out of a substance.

The compositions which exist in a proposition, however, either exist in a perfect proposition, or in an imperfect proposition. Again, with regard to the composition of an imperfect proposition, one is that of a substantive and an adjective, as "white man"; another is that of a relative and an antecedent, as "Sortes who is reading"; another is that of a nominative and an oblique case, as "the head of Sortes"; another is that of the demonstrating and the demonstrated, as "that man"; another is that of the infinitive of a verb with the accusative or some oblique case, as "to pay no heed to a man"; another is that of a verb and an adverb, as "to run swiftly"; another is that of a conjunction and of the things which it conjoins, as "Sortes and Plato"; another is that of a preposition with its variable (casuali), as "around the country-house." But these are not particularly pertinent to our topic.

Of the compositions of perfect propositions, however, one is that of a simple proposition; another is that of a compound proposition. The composition of a simple proposition is that in which only one predicate is united with one subject, or one attribute with one subject. But this is done through a verb insofar as it implies an act in a mode of being predicable of another and of tending toward an external substance. By reason of this the verb is a sign of things which are

[3] Priscian, *Institutiones Grammaticae.* Books i to xiii are edited by Henry Keil from an edition by Martin Hertz (Leipzig: B. G. Teubner, 1855), volume I. Books xiii to xviii are edited by Martin Hertz (Leipzig: B. G. Teubner, 1859), volume II. All references are to these editions of Priscian. ix, 1. 9.

predicated of another, just as a predicate is of a subject. This composition is signified by the verb but it is signified primarily in this substantive verb "is" and through the verb "is" itself in other verbs in which it is understood. Moreover this composition is found among beings, as in the case of "Man is an animal," and among non-beings, as "A chimera is a non-being"; therefore it is not being absolutely, but only being in the mind. The reference is to being or non-being according to the requirements of the extremes. Hence, whenever the substantive verb as such is predicated, as in: "Sortes is," it affirms that the thing is, not by virtue of a composition which it implies but by virtue of the very being which is signified by it. Hence, because such a composition only enjoys being through the understanding of one extreme in relation to the other, it follows that such a composition does not exist without the extremes. Since anything whatever is understood through that which gives being to the thing, Aristotle[4] says as a consequence that this verb "is" signifies a composition of a kind which is not understood without extremes. But the composition of a compound perfect proposition is one which has to be constructed of many simple propositions, some conjunction either implicitly or explicitly mediating, as in the case of hypothetical propositions and in arguments. And each of these compositions, namely, of a simple perfect proposition and of a compound perfect proposition, has to be determined through a negating negation. From what has been said it is evident that the aforementioned modes of composition sometimes are pertinent to what has been proposed. The first composition is that of an essential quality with a substance, as in the case of a substantive noun. The second composition is that of an accidental quality with a substance, as exists in the case of an adjectival noun. The third composition is that of an act distinct from an extrinsic substance, as is the case of a verb. The fourth composition is that of a united act with a united substance, as in the case of a participle. The fifth is the composition of a perfect proposition, which has been divided above.[5]

We now treat of negation. With regard to negation in general, evidently since it is multiplied in accordance with the diversity of compositions—a division opposite to the very one which is implied by negation—we must discuss negation after our discussion of composition. Negation can be taken in two ways. In one way [negation is taken] for the intention itself and in this way it is signified in the mode of substance by the noun "negation" and in the mode of an act by the verb "it is denied." But in this mode negation is signified only as conceived but not as exercised. The aforementioned terms do not make

---

[4] *De Interpretatione* 3. 16^b 22-25.   [5] Cf. p. 20.

a proposition negative, for in saying "A negation denies" we have an affirmative proposition. But a concept and an affection differ in this, that the concept is said to be that which is in the mind through some likeness, as when someone conceives any of the colors, he receives likenesses of them in the mind but not the things themselves; on the other hand, an affection or an exercise is said to be that which is truly in the mind or in the body, as when anyone is afflicted with grief, sorrow exists in the soul as a true affection; [in like manner] whenever anyone runs, running exists in the body as a true exercise affecting the body itself. In another way, negation is taken for the thing as the subject of the intention or for the thing signified. And this happens in two ways. In one way for the negative proposition and thus it is a species of proposition which is defined as follows: A negation is a statement which denies something of something; in another way it is taken for the instrument of negating, the adverb of negating, "not." In another way negation is taken for the effecting of negation, so as to divide composition. In this way negation is distinguished in a three-fold manner, namely, negating, infinitating, and privating. A privating [negation] is that which negates a form or quality (habitum) by separating it from a special subject naturally constituted to possess that form, as "blindness" negates vision by separating it from the subject which is perfected by the capacity, and "rest" negates motion in a subject naturally constituted to be moved. Therefore negation as privating implies the negation of a form with regard to its proper subject by separating it from the subject perfected [by it]. On the other hand, an infinitating negation is that which denies a quality or a special act of any term by separating some infinite substance, as "non-man," "non-running." And this is added to the term by composition. It is called the negation of a term, then, because it denies a quality or a special act of a term and it leaves only indeterminate or infinite being. But negating negation is that which negates the whole of what appears after it, induces its opposite, and disregards anything finite or infinite relevant to that which it denies: therefore "negating negation" is an excellent description. And it is added to a term or to the composition of a proposition by apposition, although sometimes it may be implied or included in some term.

It is clear then that, although any negation whatever negates some form, nevertheless all do not negate equally, because privating negation posits a finite being, namely, the subject of a capacity (habitus) which it negates; and infinitating negation disregards infinite being; but negating negation posits nothing, disregards nothing. In the second place it is evident that "blind" and "non-seeing" are different, because "blind" posits a subject perfected by vision. Therefore a stone is not

[22]

said to be "blind" but is correctly spoken of as "non-seeing," whether the negation is taken in this case as negating or infinitating, because it does not posit a subject perfected by vision; therefore a stone is well described as "non-seeing." And the same is to be said of any other privation in comparison with a negation, as "dead" and "non-living," "rest," "non-mobile," and so forth. In the third place it is evident that negation can be posited with the term in three ways: in the first way through implication, as "blind" is called "non-seeing"; "deaf," "non-hearing"; "alone," "not-with-another" (non-cum-alio); in another way through composition, as "non-man," "non-running," according as the "non" is an infinitating negation; in the third way through apposition, as "The man is not running."

Having spoken of negation in general, we must speak of negation in particular. First we must mention the negation of the infinite term which is an infinitating negation. Such a negation, however, is varied just as the terms which can be infinitated (infinitari) vary, as a substantive noun, an adjectival noun, a verb and a participle; but pronouns and the indeclinable parts of the parts of speech cannot be infinitated because of themselves they enjoy an infinite signification. Similarly, universal signs and other syncategorematic words for the same reason are never infinitated. Aristotle[6] says that negation must not be added to this sign "every," because it does not signify a universal, rather it signifies as universally as possible that which is understood with relation to an infinitating negation, but not with relation to a negating one.

Hence it must be noted that, since any affirmation whatever is opposed to its own negation, a noun can be infinitated in two ways, because in anything other than being and the other transcendentals there is a twofold composition. One kind of composition is that of differentiae in the proper genus, or if there should be specific differentiae, as are the differentiae which are added to being according to the nature of the end or of any cause, through which the supreme genera differ among themselves; for when they differ, it is necessary that they differ through something. Hence a substance is a subsisting being; quantity really is an accident measurative of substance; relation is the compared being of substance and so on. Another kind is the composition of matter and form, either truly or proportionally. And according to this the noun is sometimes infinitated from the point of view of privation. And in this way it posits being by removing the aggregation of differentiae from the first predicable. And thus there is only predicated of being that aggregation of differentiae which can be removed by one differentia alone or by many or by all. Thus

6 *De Interpret.* 10. 20ᵃ 7-13.

[23]

"non-man" and the like is said to be a privative term. In another way
a noun is infinitated from the point of view of negation. In this way
"non-man" posits nothing, is a negative term and is predicated of any
being whatever other than man and of non-being. Thus the statement
of Aristotle[7] is verified that negations are related oppositely to affirmations, so that, just as an affirmation follows in relation to a negation, so it correctly follows: "If there is a man, there is an animal" and
"If there is a non-animal, there is a non-man." And what has been said
holds true both in the case of substantial terms and accidental ones.
It must be noted, however, that in the case of general terms, as are
"being," "something," "thing," and so forth, the infinitude is found only
with respect to negation, because in these there is no twofold composition as there is in the case of specific terms. Whence "non-being,"
"non-something," and so forth is predicated only of non-being. Just
as non-man is not predicated of man, so neither is "non-being" predicated of being, since an opposite cannot be predicated of its opposite.
Further, it must be noted that a noun is infinitated not only in the
singular number but also in the plural number, as for example, "non-
men," "non-whites," because, in a negation of such a kind implying
the thing signified and its negation, either the negation happens to
the thing signified prior to the numeration and then the privation of
form follows with respect to any singular subject whatever—thus this
is false, pointing to Sortes and a small horse: "These are non-men"—
or the numeration comes first and then the supervening negation does
not deny the singulars absolutely but insofar as they are numerated,
and then the previous proposition is true, because then the meaning
is not that each of the two "is not a man" but that [each of the two is]
"not many men," and in this way a negating negation is posited.

The verb is infinitated enough by a negation added to it regarding composition, the [negation] denying the act of the verb in relation
to an intrinsic substance, as, for example, "is not running" is affirmed
of anything not included under "running"; and in the same way a
participle is infinitated by a negation destroying the composition of
an act with a united substance, by reason of the fact that the verb
and the participle agree in regard to the principal signified, as we saw
previously, when we said "non-running" has only the same meaning
as "who does not run." Though such a verb, whenever it is taken in
a proposition, may seem to be negated, nevertheless with respect to
the meaning of the word such a verb cannot remain infinite in a
proposition, for insofar as that negation can negate the intrinsic composition of the verb by denying the act in relation to an intrinsic
substance but not in relation to an extrinsic substance, as when one

[7] *De Interpret.* 6. 17ᵃ 31.

[24]

says: "Caesar is not running," in one sense it means "Caesar is not running," in another sense: "Caesar is not-running," and in this way there is an infinite verb. This composition, however, in accordance with which the verb is infinite, is still twofold according to what was said concerning an infinite noun, because either the verb is there infinitated according to negation and thus it posits nothing and can be verified with regard to being and to non-being—and in this respect Aristotle[8] says that the infinite verb belongs similarly to anything whatever, both that which is and that which is not—or it is infinitated according to privation and thus it posits being and so is not verified of non-being.

Having discussed the negation of terms, we must treat of the negation of a proposition. For a negating negation denies the composition of a proposition, because it removes the composition of an act with an extrinsic substance, which is the composition of a proposition. However, such a negation in a proposition sometimes precedes the quality and quantity of the proposition and then it negates each by positing the opposite of each, as for example, "It is not the case that every man is running" is a particular negative because it is equivalent to the following: "Some man is not running." But to be sure it sometimes precedes only the quality and so does not alter the quantity of the proposition, as for example, "Every man is not running." Hence, although a negation placed before and placed after a singular term signifies the same thing, as "Sortes is not running" and "It is not the case that Sortes is running," yet it is not the same with regard to the following terms, because this is indesignate: "Man is not running"; but "It is not the case that a man is running" is universal. And if it be said that transposed nouns and verbs signify the same thing according to Aristotle,[9] it must be said that he understands this with regard to words that are capable of functioning as subjects or predicates or [are] absolute dispositions of the subject or predicate, but he did not understand this with regard to those things which are the dispositions of one thing in relation to another, as are negations or universal signs. For a negation denies one thing of another. Sometimes such negation is absolute or independent, as in the previously mentioned examples; at other times it is included in the subject or in some sign, as "Nobody is running" or "No man is running."

With regard to what has been discussed, this sophism arises: "No man running, you are an ass." *The proof:* This is false: "Any man running, you are an ass." Therefore its contradictory is true, viz., "Not any man running, you are an ass." And because "not any" and "no" are equivalent, it follows that the initial statement is true.

[8] *De Interpret.* 3. 16[b] 15.   [9] *De Interpret.* 10. 20[b] 1.

To the contrary: "No man running, you are an ass"; therefore while no man is running, or because [no man is running], or if no man is running, you are an ass—but this is false; therefore the sophism is false.

Solution: The initial statement is absolutely false and the proof errs by division because in the case of the proposition: "Not any man running, you are an ass," the negation "not" can negate the participle only and in this way there is division and the initial statement is false, or it can negate the following verb and in this way there is composition and the initial statement is true. But in the first way it is equivalent to this: "No man running, you are an ass"; therefore that is false. And still because the negation included in the sign "No" cannot be thought of beyond the participle on account of the rule: whenever negation and distribution are included in the same term, one can be thought of in relation to nothing without the other, but distribution is not thought of beyond the participle, and therefore neither is negation, it follows that this is false: "No man running, you are an ass." And this is also false: "Not any man running, you are an ass," unless this second proposition is understood in the composite sense, as was stated.

There is, moreover, a rule that two negations mutually affecting each other are equivalent to one affirmation, as, for example, "Not every man is not running" is equivalent to "Some man is running." The cause of this is, whenever two negations precede mutually the same composition, one destroys the other. Therefore it posits the affirmation opposed to itself. Although such reflection cannot happen in the case of accidents, just as heat does not act on itself but rather on its object, still a negation, because it is a logical being, having been caused by the mind, can be reflected upon a negation or upon the negated thing. Therefore the negation "nothing" is able to negate, although it cannot be affirmed, even though such may not be the case with regard to the contraries of nature. Yet two affirmations are not equivalent to one negation by virtue of the fact that one affirmation does not destroy another but rather it strengthens it and affirms it to a greater degree. Nor is an affirmation opposed to that which it affirms, that is, the object, as for example, "A man is running" affirms that a man is running. Hence, affirmation does not destroy whatever it affirms. But negation is opposed to that which it denies. Therefore on account of the opposition it always destroys its object, as we said, with respect to one composition, since with respect to different compositions one negation does not destroy another. Nor does it posit an affirmation, since this is not an affirmative proposition: "The man, who is not running, is not moved."

Another rule is that whenever two universal negative signs are placed in the same statement, one in the subject and the other in the predicate, the first is equivalent to its own contrary and the other is equivalent to its own contradictory. But this rule holds only when the negation of one affects the negation of the other. Therefore if one of these signs should be implicative in respect to the subject, the rule does not hold. Hence these propositions are not equivalent: "No being that is nothing, is a man" and "Any being whatever which is something, is a man," because the second is false and the first is true—which is obvious because its contradictory is false, namely: "Any being whatever that is nothing, is a man."

In this connection the following sophism is considered: "Nothing is nothing." *The proof:* Its contradictory is false, namely: "Something is nothing"; therefore the initial statement is true.

To the contrary: "Nothing is nothing"; therefore nothing is no substance. But this is false because it is equivalent to: "Anything whatever is some substance," which is false. Therefore the initial statement is false.

Solution: It must be said that the initial statement is absolutely true, because by the rule stated it is equivalent to: "Anything whatever is something."

Certainly with regard to the disproof it must be said that it errs by the fallacy of accident in arguing from the superior to the inferior of the negative just as this: "Nothing is nothing" is equivalent to: "Anything whatever is something," so also this: "Nothing is no substance" is equivalent to this: "Anything whatever is some substance." Therefore just as it does not follow in the case of the propositions: " 'Anything whatever is something'; therefore 'anything whatever is some substance,' " so also it does not follow in this case: " 'Nothing is nothing'; therefore 'nothing is no substance.' "

Secondly, this rule must be noted: Whenever any negation is posited in a proposition with any syncategorematic word or even by implication, the statement is equivocal by virtue of the fact that one of these syncategorematic words can include the other or can be included by the other. And that is said to include the other which determines and is added to the other. But that is said to be included which is understood and which is determined by the other or through the other.

With regard to this, let us discuss the sophism: "Sortes runs not necessarily" (*"Sortes non currit necessario"*). *The proof:* Its contradictory is false, namely: "Sortes runs necessarily"; therefore the initial statement is true.

To the contrary: "Sortes runs not necessarily." Therefore it is nec-

[27]

essary that Sortes does not run. But this is false. Therefore the initial proposition from which it follows is false also.

Solution: One must say that the initial statement is equivocal by virtue of the fact that the negation can include the sign "necessarily" and then the negation of necessity follows, and in this way the initial statement is true, because the meaning is that this is not necessary: "Sortes runs"; in another way the necessary can include the negation, and in this way the necessity of the negation is posited, and in this sense the initial statement is false, because the meaning is this: "Sortes runs not" is necessary.

Furthermore, there is another rule which rests upon the preceding: Whenever a negation is placed before a hypothetical proposition in which there is a twofold copula the statement is twofold by virtue of the fact that the negation can negate one part absolutely, namely, that which it more immediately precedes or the principal part, if the other part is more important; it can also negate the conjunction of one with the other and this results from the fact that the negation can determine the conjunction of the hypothetical and include it, or can be determined and included by it.

The following sophism is discussed: "No man is, if some man is." *The proof:* It is not the case that Sortes is, if some man is. It is not the case that Plato is, if some man is—and so forth. Therefore the initial statement is true. That any one of the proofs is true is evident through their contradictories which are arrived at by removing the negation.

To the contrary: Because an opposite is predicated of an opposite, it follows that the statement is false and impossible.

Solution: It must be said that the initial statement is false and as to the proof the answer is that any of the proofs is ambiguous by virtue of the fact that the negation when placed before the consequent can negate it absolutely, and in this way the negation is included for the sake of a contradiction, and any one whatever of the proofs is false, and the conclusion follows, and the meaning is "It is not the case that Sortes etc.," that is, as a consequence of "some man's being" it follows that "Sortes is not"; in another way it can negate the sequence of the consequent from the antecedent, and in this way the negation includes a contradiction, and any one whatever of the proofs is true, and the meaning is "It is not the case that Sortes is, if some man is," that is, it does not follow that "If some man is, that Sortes is," and in this way the conclusion does not follow, seeing that in the premises the consequent is denied relative to the antecedent, as it ought to be denied in making a conditional negative. But in the conclusion there is an absolute negation, because the negation in the sign "No [i.e., not any]" *(nullus)* whose distribution is singular, goes beyond the composition of the consequent by reason of the fact that the distributive sign "nothing" *(nihil)* distributes beyond its own conclusion. And when negation and distribution are included in the same term, one is considered in relation to nothing without the other.

This clarifies the solution of the following sophism: "It is not the case that God is and you are an ass." *The proof:* Its contradictory is false, namely: "God is and you are an ass"; therefore the initial statement is true.

To the contrary: "It is not the case that God is and you are an ass." Therefore God is not. The second proposition is false. Therefore also the first one.

Solution: It must be said that the negation can negate absolutely the first part of the copulative and be included by the copulation, and in this way it is false, in accordance with the disproof; or it can negate that copulative and then it includes the copulation, and in this way it is true, as is proven by its own contradictory. Contradiction ought to be asserted in this way in the case of hypothetical propositions, namely, by placing the negation in front of the whole proposition.

We now discuss exclusive words. Having spoken of the negations of a proposition, we must treat of exclusive words which have within themselves the power of negation. First we must refer to exclusive words, such as "only" and "alone" which are called exclusive words, not because they signify exclusion but because they exercise it in a proposition; just as a word, generally speaking, is not called significative because it signifies its own signification, but rather because it exercises that and signifies some determinate thing. Therefore an exclusive word exercises exclusion by virtue of the fact that it signifies a privation of the association or of the concomitance of one thing with another from the point of view of some third; as a consequence of this privation of exclusion, there follows the exclusion of all other things which differ from what is included under a third thing. Hence it is clear that the proper act of an exclusive word is to exclude every other thing from what is included under a third thing. Hence whenever an exclusive word is added to a subject, it excludes whatever differs from the subject with respect to the predicate; for example, "Only Sortes runs," therefore "Nothing other than Sortes runs." But whenever it is added to the predicate, it excludes whatever differs from the predicate with respect to some subject; for example, "Sortes sees only Plato," therefore "He does not see anything other than Plato." Yet at times an exclusive word excludes something from the form of the subject and from the form of the predicate. Then it does not make a proposition exclusive but rather a proposition with an excluded subject or predicate. When one says: "Only God is," the meaning can be: "That which is God and nothing other than God has being," and in this way the proposition is true; but if it be exclusive, the meaning is: "God is and nothing other than God is," and in this way the proposition is exclusive and false.

Furthermore, four things are required for exclusion, namely, that which is excluded; that from which it is excluded or that from which the exclusion is made; that with respect to which the exclusion can exist; and the act of excluding by the exclusive word as through an instrument which implies exclusion. In the case of "Only Sortes runs" the meaning is "Sortes runs and nothing other than Sortes runs": "Sortes" is that from which the exclusion is made; "other than Sortes" is that which is excluded; "runs" is that with respect to which the exclusion is made; and "only" is the exclusive word which exercises the act of excluding.

Moreover, propositions in which exclusive words are posited, occur in four ways: in the first way, when neither exclusion nor composition is denied, for example, "Only man is an animal"; in the second way whenever exclusion alone is denied but not composition, as "Not only man is an animal," and this is the contradictory of the preceding proposition; in the third way, whenever a composition alone is denied, as "Only a stone is not an animal"; in the fourth way, whenever the exclusion and composition are denied at the same time, as "It is not the case that only a stone is not an animal," and this is the contradictory of the preceding proposition. Hence a proposition is simply exclusive only when exclusion is not denied, regardless of whether the composition is affirmed or denied.

Hence there is a rule that a simply exclusive proposition posits its prejacent and, along with this, the proposition which is expounded by the exclusion; for example, "Only man is an animal" expresses these two propositions: "Man is an animal" and "Nothing other than man is an animal." Hence an exclusive proposition is said to be a proposition taken with an exclusive sign and the prejacent (praeiacens) is that proposition which remains when the exclusive word has been removed, as is obvious in the example given. It follows then that a simply exclusive proposition is equivalent to a copulative composed of its prejacent and the proposition posited under the influence of the exclusion. Therefore the truth of the simply exclusive proposition requires the truth of both parts and for its falsity the falsity of one of them is sufficient.

Another rule: A proposition in which the exclusion is negated, does not definitely negate the prejacent nor any part of the exclusive as a whole, rather it denies only one part disjunctively in relation to the other. The reason for this is that it negates the copulation which is posited by its own contradictory and it posits a disjunction of the contradicting parts. But to negate a copulative as a whole, one part of it is not definitely negated, rather one part is negated disjunctively in relation to the other, since for its falsity the falsity of one part is sufficient indifferently.

With reference to what has been said, the following sophism is discussed: "Only one is." *Proof:* One is and nothing other than one is; therefore only one is. Boethius[10] says that everything is one because it is one in number, hence only one is. Again, there is the rule: As often as one convertible is said of the other convertible, if an exclusive word is truly connected to one, it is also connected to the other. But being and one are convertible. And also this is true: "Only being is; therefore only one is."

But *to the contrary:* Many things are; therefore "It is not the case that only one is."

Solution: One must say that the initial statement is ambiguous. Because "one" is defined as "that which is undivided being," therefore being is regarded as a subject and material with respect to unity. And undividedness is its formal nature. Therefore exclusion can be made from "unity" from the point of view of its material nature and on account of otherness. And in this way it is true, because it is equivalent to this: "Only being is." In another way, exclusion can be made from "unity" from the point of view of its formal nature and for excluding plurality. In this way the initial statement is false, as is clear from the disproof. Regarding the first two arguments, it must be said that they are true, because they accept "one" from the point of view of its material nature. Regarding the third argument stated, one must say that that rule is understood to apply whenever the two are converted in both the real and the logical order at the same time. This, however, is not true of being and of unity. Therefore, granted that this is absolutely true: "Only being is," nevertheless this is not: "Only one is," save only in one sense, as has been said.

There are, moreover, two species of exclusion, namely, the generic [or general][11] and the specific [or special](*specialis*). Generic [or general] exclusion exists whenever there is generally excluded from something everything which differs from that with respect to something [else]. In this way, the meaning of the exclusive proposition: "Only Sortes runs" is "Sortes runs and nothing other than Sortes runs."

[10] Cf. *In Porphyrium Commentariorum* iii. (PL 64, 110 A).
[11] The term "generalis" means "generic" and *"general."* The meaning of the Latin can be translated better by varying the acceptance of the term.

And thus it is not called generic [or general] exclusion by virtue of the fact that the things which differ in genus are excluded, but rather because all things in general which are different from the included are excluded. Specific [or special] exclusion exists whenever there is excluded from something only those things which agree with it in some one particular. In this way, the meaning of "Only Sortes runs" is "Sortes runs and no other man than Sortes runs." That proposition can thus be true, granted that many horses may be running along with Sortes. And it is not called specific [or special] exclusion because things which differ in species are excluded, but because some beings are excluded from something with respect to something particular.

From this it is evident that there is no numerical exclusion because every exclusion is either generic or specific. Certainly things which mutually agree in number cannot be excluded, because when it is said "Man alone runs," this posits that man runs, and if the numerically the same could be excluded, then the risible or the rational could be excluded from man and the meaning would then be: "Man alone runs," that is, "Man runs but nothing risible runs," which implies a contradiction.

Furthermore, regarding specific [or special] exclusion, the following rule is given: Whenever specific exclusion occurs, an argument from the inferior to the superior taken with an exclusive word does not hold, nor from the superior to the inferior, nor from a part of the subject nor from a part of the predicate given. Just as if Sortes and horses are running and other men are not running but rather are moved, this is true: "Sortes alone runs," by making a specific exclusion, because the meaning is: "Sortes runs but no man other than Sortes runs." Yet it does not follow that "Sortes alone runs; therefore man alone runs," because the second proposition is false in the case posited. Nor does it follow from a part of the predicate that "Sortes alone runs; therefore Sortes alone is moved," because other men are moved, although they may not be running.

Moreover, with regard to generic [or general] exclusion, the following rule is given: Whenever general exclusion occurs, it is argued validly from the inferior to the superior when there is a word which is exclusive relative to the subject, but it does not hold relative to the predicate nor, indeed, in arguing from the superior to the inferior. That it can hold relative to the subject in arguing from the inferior to the superior is obvious, because it validly follows that "Only Sortes runs; therefore man runs" from the point of view of affirmation; and from the point of view of negation it follows that "Nothing other than Sortes runs; therefore nothing other than man runs." That it cannot hold relative to the predicate nor, indeed, from the superior to the inferior is obvious, because a proposition which includes in itself [both] affirmation and negation, on account of the affirmation does not hold from the superior to the inferior, so that it does not follow that "Aristotle alone is moved; therefore Aristotle alone runs," and on account of negation it does not follow that "Aristotle alone runs; therefore Aristotle alone is moved." Whence in both such cases the fallacy of the consequent is committed.

With regard to the aforementioned, we [now] consider the following sophism: "Only the true is opposed to the false." *The proof:* The true is opposed to the false and nothing other than the true is opposed to the false; therefore only the true is opposed to the false.

To the contrary: Only the true is opposed to the false. Therefore only the true and the false are opposed. This is false because white and black are also opposed; also hot and cold.

Solution: One must say that the initial statement is absolutely true and the disproof errs in concluding from the inferior to the superior [when there is] an exclusive word [which is understood] relative to the predicate, because "the true is opposed to the false" is inferior to "opposition [taken] absolutely," just as "the opposition of the true and the false" is inferior to "opposition in general." For this must be understood, that "Only the true is opposed to the false" from the point of view of the nature of the false [itself]; for, from another viewpoint, the false can be opposed to the false.

Whence there is the rule: Whenever an exclusive word is added to any term including a subject (*suppositum*) and an accident, or the material and the formal, the statement is ambiguous because it can make the exclusion with respect to itself from the point of view of the subject or from the point of view of the accident, or from the point of view of the matter or from the point of view of the form—just as we said above concerning the [proposition]: "Only one is."

But with regard to that which is excluded, the following rule is given: An exclusive word added to any term, excludes everything which is different from it as far as natural supposition [is concerned]. For anything is different from another in two ways: in one way according to the essence and natural supposition at the same time, for example, "man" and "horse"; in another way according to natural supposition only, as "man" and "chimera." For although "chimera" may not be different from "man" from the point of view of essence, nevertheless it is different from it from the point of view of natural supposition. For not only beings are denoted by the term but also non-beings.

From this rule it follows, first, that an exclusive word added to being or to anything convertible with being, excludes something, because it excludes from being everything else which differs from it according to natural supposition. But supposition relates not only to being but also to non-being. Therefore, when it is added to being, non-beings are excluded. And if it be said that an exclusive word can exclude nothing except what is outside the term to which it is added, but outside of being there is nothing, therefore, added to being, it excludes nothing, and conceding that something can be understood by reason outside of real being, not however outside of being in general, as it extends itself to real being and to logical being, one must say that although being is understood universally for real being and for logical being, nevertheless something can always be understood which is outside it as far as reason is concerned, because the non-being opposed to it can always be grasped by reason; and this [is] on account of the infinite reflection of reason upon its own acts, for, given any being of reason whatever, reason itself can negate that and understand its opposite. Therefore outside of being understood in any way whatever something different can be understood according to natural supposition but not according to reality.

In the second place, it follows that, if the most universal genera are understood concretely, an exclusive word added to one does not always exclude another, for example, it does not follow [that] "Only an active [being] runs; therefore a grammarian runs," or "a musician," "a tricubital [being]," or "a man," by virtue of the fact that a running Sortes can be a grammarian, a musician, a tricubital [being], a man and an active [being]. But if those genera are understood abstractly, this is ambiguous, for either they are taken as absolutely different, or as being in one mode in functioning as subject for another, as when one [thing] is a subject for another, or in functioning as predicate, insofar as it belongs to one [thing to be] in another. If they are understood as being in one mode in functioning as a subject or an inherent, the exclusive word added to one still does not exclude the other; for example, it does not validly follow [that] "Only a substance is colored; therefore a surface is not," because a substance and a surface exist as one subject of color. If they are understood in the abstract and as they are different, the exclusive word added to one most universal genus, excludes every other, for example, it validly follows [that] "Only substance is; therefore quantity or quality [is] not." But if it be said: an exclusive word never excludes that which is understood in the subject to which it is added—as when one says "Only white [is]," body is not excluded: rather, on the contrary, quantity causes [one] to understand substance; therefore in saying "Only quantity is," substance is not excluded—one must say that one [thing] is included in another in three ways. In one way essentially, as animal in man; but such is

[34]

not excluded, as it does not follow [that] "Only man runs; therefore animal does not run." In another way, one [thing] is included in another as a subject in the case of a concrete accident; but still in that way, that which is understood in another, is not excluded, as "Only white [is]; therefore body [is] not." In the third way, something is included in another which is nevertheless different from it with respect to being, as an effect in its cause and a cause in [its] effect or a relative in a correlative. But in this way an exclusive word added to one excludes the other by reason of the fact that they exist as different subjects (supposita), provided that substance is understood in the case of quantity understood abstractly, as a cause in an effect. Hence it follows [that] "Only quantity [is]; therefore substance [is] not." However in the case of the [proposition] "Only quantity is," two things are included, namely, that substance is and that it is not, because in positing that quantity is, one posits that substance is and yet one posits that substance is not by the exclusive word. Therefore that [proposition] "Only quantity is," is impossible because it posits two contradictories at the same time.

In the third place, it follows that an exclusive word added to a species of one category excludes the species of another category provided they do not constitute one subject or unless one is contained in the other. Hence, in general, there are five exclusions. The first is a different subject, as "Only Sortes; therefore not Plato." The second is a different place, as "Only here; therefore not there." The third is a different time, as "Only today; therefore not yesterday." The fourth is the opposite from the point of view of the predicate, as "Only white; therefore not black." The fifth is a different accident posited in the predicate, because, when one does not include the other or does not belong to the other, the other is always excluded; as "Sortes is only a grammarian; therefore not a musician and running"; but it does not follow that "He is only a grammarian; therefore he is not a cleric or intelligent." Through this it is clear that an exclusive word added to a species of one category excludes the other species of the same category, save where one species is necessarily included in the other, as a lesser number in a greater, or a line in a surface or a body, for in such cases this does not follow: "Only a surface; therefore not a line."

In the fourth place it follows that an exclusive word added to one of the opposites in any genus whatever of opposition excludes the other, because two opposites do not constitute one subject but rather different ones; now the rule is: whenever some things do not constitute one subject, an exclusive word added to one always excludes the other, as "Only white; therefore not black."

In connection with the foregoing, the sophism is discussed: "If only a father is, it is not the case that only a father is." *The proof:* If only a father is, a father is, because the exclusive word posits its prejacent. But if a father is, a child is. Therefore something other than a father is. Hence, "If only a father is, it is not the case that only a father is."

To the contrary: In this case an opposite is seen to follow from an opposite; therefore the statement is impossible.

[Solution:] One must say that the initial statement is true because it is a conditional whose consequent follows by necessity from the antecedent, which is sufficient for the truth of a conditional. For the antecedent, namely: "Only a father is," posits that a child is inasmuch as it posits that a father is, and it posits that a child is not because of the exclusion, for it excludes anything different from the father; therefore it posits that a child is and that a child is not. And thus it posits both parts of a contradiction. Therefore in this case one part of a contradiction follows from a proposition which includes the contradiction as a whole, just as any part of a copulative follows from a copulative as a whole. In regard to the disproof it is said that in that case an opposite does not follow from an opposite but one part of a contradiction follows from an antecedent which includes each of its two parts.

Regarding the above, this sophism is discussed: "It is possible that Sortes sees only every man not seeing himself." *The proof:* It is possible that Sortes sees only one blind man; but every blind man is a man not seeing himself; therefore it is possible that Sortes sees only every man not seeing himself.

To the contrary: If "It is possible that Sortes etc." is posited as consisting in this, that Sortes should see only every man not seeing himself, then either Sortes sees himself or he does not. If he does not see himself, then there is a man not seeing himself; therefore he does not see every man not seeing himself. If he sees himself, then he does not see only a man not seeing himself.

Solution: This is impossible: "Sortes sees only every man not seeing himself." This is clear, because it is equivalent to these two propositions: "Sortes sees only every man not seeing himself" and "Sortes does not see some man seeing himself." And these two are its exponents. But from this: "Sortes does not see some man seeing himself," this follows: "Sortes does not see himself," because, if he were to see himself, he would see some man seeing himself. But from this: "Sortes does not see himself," taken along with the first of the exponents, the other part of the contradiction follows, in saying: "Sortes sees only every man not seeing himself; but he himself is one not seeing himself, therefore he is one seeing himself." Therefore the initial statement

[36]

includes these two contradictories: "Sortes sees himself" and "Sortes does not see himself." Therefore it is impossible. And also the following: "It is possible that a substance sees only every man not seeing himself."

The proof is truly guilty of a *non sequitur* in arguing from the inferior to the superior with distribution and with an exclusive word relative to the predicate, because "a man not seeing himself" is superior to "a blind man" because a man sleeping or having closed eyes is "not seeing himself," yet he still is not "blind." And yet it is argued: It is possible that "a blind man" and "one not seeing for some time" are convertible—and again: It is possible that Sortes sees only a blind man, therefore "It is possible that he sees only every man not seeing himself." But it must be known that each of these, considered by itself, is possible; but both however are not possible at the same time, that "a blind man" and "a man not seeing" should be convertible and that "Sortes sees only every man not seeing himself."

Furthermore it is a rule that an exclusive word added to an integral whole with respect to accidents, which only belong to the whole itself, can exclude parts; for example, it validly follows that "Only the house weighs a hundred pounds; therefore not the wall." But with respect to accidents which are able to belong to the whole and the parts or with respect to those accidents which can only belong to one, an exclusive word added to the whole does not exclude the parts; for example, it does not validly follow that "Only the house is white; therefore the wall is not white."

There is another rule: An exclusive word added to a part always excludes its whole, with the exception of the universal whole and the whole in kind. The rule holds with respect to an integral part, to a quantitative part, to a spatial part, to a temporal part, and to a numerical part; for example, it validly follows that: "Only the wall is white; therefore not the whole house" and "There are only ten categories; therefore not twelve."

Regarding what has been said above, this sophism is discussed: "Whatever differs from Sortes alone is not Sortes or a part of Sortes." *The proof:* Whatever differs from Sortes is not Sortes or a part of Sortes; but not from another than Sortes; therefore etc.

To the contrary: Whatever differs from Sortes alone is not Sortes, etc.; but Plato is not Sortes or a part of Sortes; therefore Plato differs from Sortes alone.

Solution: The initial statement is false, as is clear from the disproving reason. In regard to *the proof* one answers that one of the proving statements is false, namely: "But not from another than Sortes," etc. And if it be asked from which other, it must be said that the question is a poor one, for that ablative "another" *(alio)* is not understood as standing for one thing but for many in general. Just as when one has posited that any man whatever sees his own horse, only "Every man sees a horse" is true. One must not however ask which horse, because this accusative stands not for one determinate horse but for many in general.

There is also this rule: Whenever an exclusive word is added to any statement, the statement is ambiguous by virtue of the fact that the exclusive word can exclude either in relation to the statement as a whole or in relation to the subject of the statement itself.

Regarding these remarks, this sophism is discussed: "That only God be God is necessary." *The proof:* That God be God is necessary and nothing other than God be God is necessary; therefore the initial statement is true.

To the contrary: "That only God be God is necessary"; therefore that man be or not be is not necessary. But this is false.

Solution: It must be said that the initial statement is ambiguous by reason of the fact that this word "only" can exclude the whole expression, "God be God," and thus it is composite and false; as is clear from the disproof, because it posits that no other expression is necessary save this: "God be God": in another way it can exclude from the subject of the expression, and thus it is divided and true, for the meaning is "That God be God is necessary and nothing other than God to be God is necessary."

Another rule follows: Whenever two syncategorematic words, each determining the other, are posited in the same statement, or one syncategorematic word is posited twice, being able to determine itself, the statement is ambiguous by reason of the fact that one can determine the other and vice versa. For this reason, the ancients were accustomed to say that one can include the other or be included by the other.

Regarding what has been said above, this sophism is discussed: "In relation to three alone two alone are fewer." *The proof:* In relation to three, two alone are fewer; and to no others than three, two alone are fewer; therefore the initial statement is true.

To the contrary: In relation to three alone two alone are fewer; therefore to three alone two are fewer. But this is false.

Solution: The initial statement is ambiguous because the exclusion posited in the oblique case can determine the other posited in the nominative case and then it is expounded through the exclusion existing in the oblique case; and in this way it is true as is evident from the proof: in another way the exclusion posited in the nominative case can determine the other and so it is expounded through the exclusion posited in the nominative case; but in this way it is false, because one

[38]

of its exponents is false, namely, "In relation to three alone two are fewer," since two are fewer than all other numbers in an ascending order. In speaking of the ascent of quantity which belongs to number, notice that the ascent is of two sorts, namely, the quantitative ascent or the increase which occurs in proceeding from a smaller number to a larger, and in this respect the larger numbers are always the superior; another is the causal ascent, thus the numbers closer to unity (which is the cause of all numbers) are always superior.

From the aforementioned rule it is obvious that this exclusive proposition is ambiguous: "Only necessaries are true necessarily," because the sign "only" can in one way determine "necessarily" and in this way the proposition is composite and true, because the meaning is that "Necessaries are true necessarily"; in another way this mode "necessarily" can determine it and thus the proposition is divided and false, because the meaning is: "Only necessaries are true and this necessarily." But this is false because some contingencies are true. On this account the original proposition can easily be proved and disproved.

Further, it is evident that this is certainly ambiguous: "Sortes only is white or black," because in one way "only" can determine that disjunction and in this way there is a proposition with a predicate taken disjunctively, and it is false, because the meaning is: "Sortes is white or black and no one other than Sortes"—which is false; in another way the disjunction can determine the exclusion and thus the proposition can be true—it having been supposed that "Sortes may be white and no other"—because the meaning is: "Sortes only is white or Sortes only is black" and one part of that disjunction is true.

Regarding the act of excluding and the exclusive signs it must be known that "only" (tantum) and "alone" (solus) differ as follows in their exclusions, because "alone" always excludes from something accidental, whether it is posited in the subject or in the predicate: for example, "Sortes alone runs," that is, "Sortes and no other"; and in the predicate, as "I give a denarius alone," that is, "I give a denarius and nothing else." But this word "only" sometimes excludes from some one act by neglecting to consider the remaining acts; as when one says: "Sortes is only reading," that is, "Sortes is reading and he is doing nothing else." But to the contrary: This word "only" is an adverb, therefore it always excludes from some act because an adverb has to determine a verb. One must answer that the characterizing qualification (dispositio) of a substance is twofold: one, of course, is that which characterizes a substance absolutely and immediately, as "white" and "black"; and the other is that which characterizes a substance, an act mediating—for example, when one says: "He attacks the proud," the word "proud" bespeaks the pride which belongs to a substance, an act mediating, or through an act. Similarly then there is a dual characterizing qualification of an act. One determines an act absolutely and determinately or immediately, as "well," "badly," "swiftly," and so on; and such a characterizing qualification always determines the act or the verb. Another is that which determines the act, a substance mediating, as "only," "merely," "alone," "peculiarly"; but such characterizing qualifications sometimes determine an act immediately, but at other times with some substance mediating. Whenever they determine, with some substance mediating, they can exclude from something accidental. If it be asked whether "alone" can restrict the word to which it is connected, as a consequence of the rule: Every adjective, neither restricting nor having the power of amplifying, connected in the same way to a more general term, restricts the general term to which it is added, one must answer that "alone" does not properly restrict and that the rule ought to be understood with regard to adjectives affirming absolute and specific characterizing qualifications, such as "white" or "black," but not with regard to adjectives which indicate referential characterizing qualifications, as do "alone," "no one," nor with regard to adjectives affirming general characterizing qualifications, as "intelligible," "conjectural," and so forth.

Regarding what has been said above, this sophism is discussed: "Sortes alone is excluded," the supposition having been made that Sortes alone is excluded from some subject with respect to some predicate. *The proof:* Sortes is excluded and no one other than Sortes is excluded; therefore Sortes alone is excluded.

To the contrary: This is the kind of exclusive in which all others than Sortes are excluded; therefore it is not the case that "Sortes alone is excluded."

Solution: The initial statement is true, as is obvious from the reason given in the proof. And to the disproof one must reply that although in the proposition in which "Sortes alone is excluded," all others than Sortes are excluded, nevertheless it itself is not affirmed of itself but of one other proposition in which "Only Sortes is excluded."

Again, let it be supposed that Sortes alone knows this assertible: "a horse to be an animal," but he along with Plato and others knows many other assertibles. Then with regard to this, this sophism is discussed: "Sortes alone knows some assertible of which not everyone other than Plato is ignorant." *The proof:* Sortes knows some assertible of which another than Plato is ignorant. Either therefore everyone other or not. If everyone other, then he himself does not know that assertible which he himself knows. If not everyone other, then the initial statement is true.

To the contrary: Another than Sortes knows some assertible of which not every man other than Plato is ignorant, just as you may know one out of those generally held; therefore it is not the case that "Sortes alone knows some assertible etc."

Solution: The initial statement is true, as is obvious from the reason given in the proof. With regard to the disproof one answers that these two propositions are not contradictory: "Another than Sortes knows some assertible of which not everyone other than Plato is ignorant" and "Not another than Sortes knows some assertible of which not everyone other than Plato is ignorant," because the predicate "some assertible" is not held in the same way in both propositions. For in the case of the first proposition it is restricted by the following implication to an assertible known by others than Sortes; but in the second it is restricted to an assertible which is known only by Sortes, namely, "a horse to be an animal," because the relative "another" in this case stands only for Sortes. But if it were to stand for the same in both propositions, then these would be contradictories.

Regarding what has been said, this sophism is discussed: "Sortes alone and two are three." *The proof:* Sortes, not with another, and two are three; therefore Sortes and two are three.

To the contrary: Another than Sortes and two are three; therefore it is not the case that Sortes alone and two are three.

Solution: The initial statement is ambiguous by reason of the fact that the word "alone" can be held in one way categorematically, as "only" signifies the same as "not with another," and thus the initial statement is true as was proven, because the sense is "Sortes, not with another, and two are three"; in another way it can be held exclusively and syncategorematically, but thus it is false as was proven, because the sense is: "Sortes and two are three but nevertheless not another than Sortes and two are three." One should speak in a similar fashion of this: "Not only from 'Sortes is' does 'Sortes is' follow," because if "only" were held categorematically, as is an absolute adjective, then it is true; but if it were held exclusively, so as to effect general exclusion, then it is false. "Not only from 'Sortes is' does 'Sortes is' follow" but, along with this, it follows from "every man is" or from "every animal is" and so forth.

Having discussed exclusive words, we must discuss exceptive words, such as "with the exception of," "but," and "except." They are called exceptive words not because they signify exception, for according to this the noun "exception" and the verb "except" would be exceptive words, since they would signify exception, which is false;

[41]

rather they are called exceptive words because they exercise exception. Just as words are called exclusive, not because they signify exclusion, but because they exercise it, so exceptive words exercise exception in a proposition. Whence they signify the extraction of a part from a whole with respect to some predicate, in relation to which extraction or separation, the exception of a part from a whole, which is the proper act of an exceptive word, follows. For exception is the extraction of a part from a whole with respect to some predicate. Therefore, exceptive words are said "to except," that is, "to take without," because they denote that a part is extracted or separated from a whole, not absolutely but with respect to some predicate. From this it is clear that the exceptive word is an instance opposed to the whole and that it implies a separation. Still it is different than an exclusive word because an exclusive word affirms the separation of some whole from a part with respect to some predicate, as, for example, when one says "Only man is risible," that is, "Man and nothing other than man." But an exceptive word affirms the separation of a part from a whole, for example, in the case of "Every animal except man is irrational," man is separated from its whole. Four things are required for exception, namely, the part which is excepted; that from which the exception is made; that with respect to which an exception is made; and the exceptive word by which the exception is made as by an instrument of the excepting mind—for example, when one says "Every man except Sortes runs," "Sortes" is the part which is excepted; "every man" is the whole from which he is excepted; "runs" is that with respect to which an exception is made; and "except" is the exceptive word by which the exception is made.

Regarding that which is excepted, there is this rule: An exceptive word excepts a part which actually exists in its whole. The reason is that exception is the extraction of something from something. But wherever there is an extraction, there is actually something which is removed and something which is left; but that which is removed by leaving the rest is actually a part and that from which it is removed is the whole. Nor can that which exists only potentially be extracted from the rest. Therefore an exceptive word only excepts a part which actually exists in a whole and it affirms the customary relation of a part which actually exists in a whole to its whole. Therefore all the following propositions are absurd and false: "Every horse, except Sortes, runs" and "Man, except for Sortes, runs"; [they are absurd and false] because the excepted is not actually a part of that from which the exception is made; wherefore the exceptive word does not involve the customary relation which it requires. Although Sortes may be a part of "man," nevertheless he does not actually belong in the supposition of "man" unless a universal sign is added to "man." Therefore, it does not follow: "Man runs; therefore Sortes runs."

Another rule follows that the excepted ought always to be contained actually in that from which it is excepted and to be removed from this with respect to some third, as "Every man, except Sortes, runs."

Also, there is another rule: Whenever in any proposition as many things are excepted as are denoted, the statement is false and impossible; for example, this is false: "Every non-man except a non-man runs." The reason is that in this case the excepted does not enjoy the nature of a part and so the exceptive word does not except a part as it requires. Also, in this case the predicate is affirmed of any man whatever and it is removed from any man whatever; therefore it posits the contradictory at the same time.

Regarding what has been said above, this sophism is discussed: "Every man sees every man except himself." Let it be assumed that any man whatever can see anyone other than himself but he cannot see himself. *The proof:* Sortes sees every man except himself; and Plato sees every man except himself, and so forth; therefore the initial statement is true.

To the contrary: In that proposition as many are excepted as are denoted, because the relative "himself" is a relative of identity which is referred to the whole "every man"; wherefore it refers itself to and it stands for "every man"; wherefore the initial statement is false.

Solution: The initial statement is absolutely true, as is obvious from the proof. And in relation to the disproof one answers that that rule is understood concerning exception alone when some things are excepted in the same way as they are denoted. This is not the case here, however, for in the antecedent all men are denoted in the composite but they are not thus excepted in the reciprocal relative. Rather they are excepted individually and under a division representing individuals singularly.

Another rule is: A wholly false proposition cannot be verified regarding an exception but a proposition which is false for many can be verified regarding an exception. For example, "Every stone is a man" cannot be verified regarding an exception because it is wholly false and as many are excepted as are denoted. And this rule is posited in another way as follows: Opposite the wholly false there is no instance to be given, that is, the wholly false cannot be verified regarding an exception. A wholly false proposition is one whose contrary is true, as for example, these: "Every man is a stone" and "Every man is an ass," whose contraries are absolutely true.

Regarding what has been said, this sophism is discussed: "Every animal except man is irrational." *The proof:* This is false: "Every animal

[43]

is irrational." And there is no instance but for man. Therefore, an exception having been made for man, the proposition will be true.

To the contrary: Every animal except man is irrational. Therefore every animal except this man is irrational. But this is false.

Solution: The initial statement is true and the proof holds. But the disproof errs by a fallacy of figure of speech, by passing from simple to personal supposition, because the accusative "man" after the exceptive word has simple supposition in the first proposition and [has] personal supposition in the second proposition when it is said: "Every animal except this man etc." Further, there is a concluding from the inferior to the superior with distribution, because in: "Every animal except man," "animal" is distributed for animals other than man, and it is likewise distributed for animals other than this man in: "Every animal except this man." Therefore it is distributed for more in the second expression than in the first. And thus there is a fallacy of the consequent. Furthermore, the same judgment holds with respect to these sophisms: "Every animal except the healthy is sick"; "Every quantity except the continuous is discrete"; "Every body except the animate is inanimate"; "Every assertible except the true is false."

Regarding that from which an exception is made, the rule is posited that the exceptive word only excepts from some determinate and actual multitude. For multitude is ambiguous: one kind is indeterminate and potential; but another is determinate. But there are five types of indeterminate multitude, because one kind is the indeterminate multitude implied by a noun of plural number, as "Men run"; another is implied by a collective noun, as "The crowd is excited"; another is implied by a distributive sign multiplying a term for some subjects only, as "Infinite men run"; another is implied by a universal whole which is only potential, as "Man runs"; another [is implied] by a whole in kind, as "Man runs." In this case "man," by comparison with the parts, is regarded as a whole in kind and it posits a potential multitude. But from these types of multitude no exception is made. Therefore all of these are incongruous: "Men except Sortes run" and so forth.

Again, a determinate and actual multitude occurs in five ways. One exists in the case of a quantitative whole; another exists in the case of a spatial whole; another exists in the case of a temporal whole; another exists in the case of an integral whole; and another exists in the case of a numerical whole. From these five types an exception can well be made, as is obvious inductively from examples: from a quantitative whole, for example: "Every man except Sortes runs"; from a spatial whole, for example: "The sun shines everywhere except here"; from a temporal whole, for example: "Sortes will always run except for tomorrow"; from an integral whole, for example: "The whole house is white except the wall"; from a numerical whole, for example: "Ten except one are nine." Since in these cases there sometimes is an actual multitude and since an exception does not occur in the case of the other five types, the aforementioned rule is therefore clear, that an exception is made only from an actual and determinate multitude. This is proven in another way, because—as was previously said—the exceptive word always requires a part actually existing in the whole, which it excepts from the whole. Therefore, when it separates some part, it leaves another part in the whole, because as many cannot be excepted as are denoted. Because there are many parts actually, the exceptive word, as a consequence, always excepts from a multitude of parts actually existing in their whole.

Regarding what has been said, this sophism is discussed: "Every man except Sortes is excepted." Let it be assumed that all others apart from Sortes are excepted with respect to some predicate but not Sortes. *The proof:* This is false: "Every man is excepted." And there is no instance except for Sortes. Therefore, an exception having been made of Sortes, the proposition will be true. Therefore the initial statement is true.

To the contrary: In this proposition the exceptive word is joined to Sortes. Therefore, it excepts him with respect to the predicate. And thus Sortes is excepted. Therefore the initial statement is false.

Solution: The initial statement is true in the case posited, as is clear from the proof. And as to the disproof one answers that although in "Every man except Sortes is excepted," Sortes is excepted with respect to that predicate "is excepted," nevertheless in the other proposition only the others apart from Sortes are excepted with respect to that predicate but Sortes is not. The proposition is affirmed with regard to that but not with respect to itself. Or it can be asserted that in that case Sortes is excepted from the exception; but to be excepted from the exception is only to be excepted relatively but not absolutely, as to be deprived of by a privation is to be deprived of relatively but not absolutely.

With regard to what has been said, this sophism is discussed: "The whole of Sortes except his foot can be contained in the chest." Let it be assumed that the whole of Sortes can be placed in the chest but his foot cannot go in with him. *The proof:* In relation to the initial statement, this is false: "Sortes can be wholly placed in the chest." And there is no instance except for the foot. Therefore, an exception having been made for the foot, the initial statement will be true. Therefore this is true: "The whole of Sortes except his foot can be contained in the chest."

To the contrary: The foot can be contained in the chest since the whole is contained there; therefore it is not the case that "The whole of Sortes except his foot can be contained in the chest."

Solution: The initial statement is true and the proof holds. But the disproof errs by the fallacy of accident because an exception is made from the whole with respect to the predicate for a twofold reason. In one way because the part as such is not truly a subject to the predicate, as in the case of "Every animal except man is irrational." In another way, the part is excepted because although as such it receives the predicate, nevertheless it does not receive it with the whole or according as it is in the whole. As the case really is, the foot of Sortes as such can be contained in the chest, but not with him as a whole, still the inference is made that if the foot of Sortes can be contained in the chest with him as a whole, [then] also the whole. Therefore in this case there is a fallacy of accident.

This sophism is considered: "Ten except for five are five." *The proof:* This is false: "Ten are five." And there is no instance except for five. Therefore, an exception of five having been made, it will be true. Therefore the initial statement will be true.

To the contrary: Ten except for five are five. Therefore five are not five, because, in an exceptive affirmative proposition, the predicate is always removed from the excepted. But in the case of a negative the opposite happens, because the predicate is removed from that from which the exception is made and it is attributed to the excepted. And it ought always to be removed from the one and attributed to the other.

Solution: The initial statement is true and the proof holds. But the disproof errs by a fallacy of accident, because although five may be truly predicated of five as such, nevertheless it may not be predicated of five according as it is contained in ten. Therefore, it does not follow that "Ten except for five are five; therefore five are not five," just as it does not follow that "I do not know the one who is coming; therefore I do not know Coriscus as such, who, however, is the one who is coming."

Moreover in relation to the affirmation that in an exceptive affirmative proposition the predicate is removed from the excepted, one must say that it is only true when falsity is caused in a proposition by the excepted part in virtue of the fact that the predicate does not belong to the part as such. But when the falsity is caused by the part to which the predicate cannot belong, as is the case with its whole, but [to which] it can [belong] as such, it is not necessary that the predicate as such be removed from the excepted. And this is the case with what has been proposed. In the first way the exceptive word is

[46]

held exceptively only but in the second way it is held exceptively and restrictively at the same time. The meaning can be: "Ten except for five are five," that is, "Ten restricted by five are five."

Let this be the rule regarding exceptive words: whenever an exception is made from a quantitative whole posited in the subject, and the proposition can be universal, as when one says "Every man except Sortes runs." But whenever an exception is made from a quantitative whole posited in the predicate, or from a spatial whole, from a temporal whole, from an integral whole, or from a numerical whole, the proposition can have to do with any quantity whatever, because the subject can be held universally, particularly, indefinitely, and singularly, as can be seen concerning all of these by examples.

Another rule is: Whenever an exception is made from a quantitative whole or from one including it virtually, a subsumption can be made under the exceptive proposition and one can syllogize from that, for example, in saying: "Every man except Sortes runs; Plato is a man other than Sortes; therefore Plato runs." From this it is clear that the exceptive word posited in the major premise ought not to be repeated in the minor premise. And the reason is that the exceptive word is not an absolute qualification but a relative qualification, namely, of the subject insofar as it is the subject and of the predicate insofar as it is the predicate. Such qualifications ought not to be reiterated with the second proposition because the receptive word still includes virtually a certain restriction of the quantitative whole to which it is added. Therefore, in syllogizing, some restriction ought to be posited in the minor premise which causes that quantitative whole which is restricted by an exception to be held for others than the excepted, just as it was stated above that "Plato is a man other than Sortes," because "except" includes the restriction "other than Sortes."

Many rules follow from what has been said. The first rule is: An exceptive word does not cause the word to which it is added to be constant, because deduction to the particulars can be made under it, as it has been said. The second rule is: The antecedent of any true exceptive proposition is false but it is made true through the exception. The antecedent, moreover, of the exceptive proposition is that from which falsity is removed by the exceptive word; for example, "Every animal is irrational" is the antecedent of the true exceptive: "Every animal except man is irrational." Another rule is: Certainly if any exceptive proposition is false in part, it can be made true by an exception, but not if it will have been wholly false, as we saw previously.

In this regard, this sophism is discussed: "Sortes sees every man twice excepting Plato." Let it be assumed that in one case Sortes will have seen every man and in another case he had seen all others than

[47]

Plato. *The proof:* This is false: "Sortes sees every man." And there is no exception except for Plato. Therefore, an exception having been made for Plato, the proposition will be true. Therefore the sophism is true.

To the contrary: Sortes sees every man twice excepting Plato. Therefore twice he does not see Plato. Therefore neither in the first case nor in the second does he see Plato. But this is false.

Solution: The initial statement is ambiguous by virtue of the fact that the determinant "twice" can determine the word "excepting" and can presuppose it. In this way it is false, because the meaning is: "Sortes sees every man except Plato; and this twice," and then it follows that in no case will he have seen Plato. In another way that determinant "excepting" can determine the adverb "twice," so that the adverb "twice" determines the verb as such but not the whole sequent. In this way the proposition is true, because the meaning is: "Sortes twice sees [every] man other than Plato but he does not twice see Plato," therefore generally speaking an exception is made for Plato. In the first way a duality of exception is posited. In the second way an exception from a duality is posited.

With regard to what has been said, this sophism is discussed: "Any ten whatever excepting one are nine." *The proof:* This ten excepting one are nine; that ten etc., and so forth; therefore the initial statement is true.

To the contrary: Any ten whatever excepting one are nine. Therefore any ten other than one denarius are nine. But this is false.

Solution: The initial statement is ambiguous in that an exception can be made from that term "ten" from the point of view of integral parts and thus the proposition is true and the proof holds; in another way an exception can be made from the point of view of subjective parts but thus it is false, as is clear from the disproof. It is clear then that there is this rule: As often as a quantitative whole follows from an integral whole, [any] exception can except from it from the point of view of integral parts or from the point of view of subjective parts. But in this way the proposition is false, as is clear from the disproof. If an exception is made from the point of view of subjective parts, then such a statement is always ambiguous—as we have seen.

Let this be the rule regarding words making an exception: The word "except" is always construed with the accusative case and it makes an exception in the accusative. The reason is that "except" is a preposition devoted to the accusative case. And if one argues: "This word 'except' implies a relating with respect to an act; therefore it is an adverb, since it has the power to determine the verb; and so it is not a preposition," it must be said that adverbs and prepositions differ among themselves as follows. Because adverbs directly affirm a determination of the act of the verb, they are therefore *ad*verbs, as it were, placed next to verbs; for example, when one says "He runs swiftly," "swiftly" in this case directly describes the kind of running and a determination. But prepositions affirm a relating of the substance signified in the oblique case to the act of the verb; for example, when one says: "That one runs with swiftness," this preposition "with" affirms the relating of "swiftness" to running. Therefore, although the same thing is signified in saying "He runs swiftly" and "He runs with swiftness," nevertheless this is done in different ways. For when one says: "It passes through them," that is, "That is moved through that part," that is, "A heavenly voice was raised in that place," that is, "From heaven divinely from God" and so forth, the preposition in them always affirms a relating of a substance to the act of the verb and the adverb affirms a determination of the act of the verb. Therefore, although this word "except" may affirm a relating to the act of a verb, it does not follow as a consequence that it is an adverb.

Likewise, it is argued that it may have the power to be construed with the nominative case: because "except" removes the personal verb from the excepted, but the personal verb is only removed from the nominative, it follows that "except" ought to be construed with the nominative. It must be said that the verb is removed in two ways from some variable *(ab aliquo casuali)*: in one way directly, by removing the relating of one to another, and in this way the verb is removed from the nominative by a negation, as "I do not run," "You do not run"; in another way indirectly and consequentially, as by destroying the act as such or the subject as such or some part of it, and in this way the predicate is removed consequentially from the excepted by the exceptive word because in the first place the word "except" extracts a part from a whole with respect to something which is posited in the whole from which the exception is made, as for example: "Every man except Sortes runs."

Thirdly, since an act affirmed of a subject does not reveal a part excepted from a whole, the remotion then of the act from the excepted part follows as a consequence. Just as when anyone sees rain coming, first he removes a book from the window; secondly the rain falls on the window; thirdly the remotion of the rain from the book follows because it does not fall on the book.

From these remarks, it is clear that this word "with the exception of" *(praeter)* differs from the words "except" *(praeterquam)* and "but" *(nisi)* because "with the exception of" *(praeter)* always excepts in the accusative [case] but "except" *(praeterquam)* and "but" *(nisi)* always except in the same case in which the whole from which an exception

[49]

is made is, as for example, "No man runs except *(praeterquam)* Sortes" or "but *(nisi)* Sortes"; or "I pity no one but *(nisi)* Sortes," or "except *(praeterquam)* Sortes"; or "I speak to no man except *(praeterquam)* Sortes" or "but *(nisi)* Sortes"; or "I see no man except *(praeterquam)* Sortes" or "but *(nisi)* Sortes"; or "It is read by no man except *(praeterquam)* Sortes" or "but *(nisi)* Sortes." However these three words agree in everything else in making an exception, because they can make an exception in a similar way.

Having treated of exceptive words, logically we must [now] consider consecutive words, of such a type as is the word "if" *(si)*. They are called consecutive words not because they signify consecution because then the noun "consecution" and the verb "follows as a consequence" *(consequor)* would be consecutive words; rather they are called consecutive words because they exercise consecution so that the word "if" does not directly signify consecution but rather it exercises and signifies causality and antecedence and it exercises consecution. In the first place it certainly signifies causality, hence it is called a causal conjunction. Because it antecedes the effect, it therefore as a consequence signifies antecedence which is the condition of an antecedent in relation to a consequent; hence it is always adjoined to the antecedent. And because an antecedent and a consequent are said to be correlatives in relation to signifying antecedence, it therefore exercises consecution. In denoting the causality of an antecedent with respect to a consequent, it denotes the dependence of the consequent on the antecedent. For the antecedent can be the cause of the consequent in two ways. In one way relative to that which is: for example, when one says: "Man is rational; therefore man is risible," rational[ity] is the cause of risibility. In another way it can be the cause of the consequent relative to an inference, in considering the consequent inasmuch as it is the consequent; for example, when one says: "If man is a horse, man is irrational," "to be a horse" in this case is not the cause of "irrational," but rather vice versa. In this way it denotes causality, but not in the first way. Therefore, just as it is said that "if" implies the cause of the consequence but not of the consequent, so also it must be understood that it does not affirm the causality of the consequent in accordance with that which is when it is said that it affirms the cause of the consequent and of the consequence insofar as it is the consequent.

But sometimes this conjunction "if" affirms only a possible or probable condition, for example: "If you will come to me, I will give you a horse"; sometimes, to be sure, it affirms a necessary condition, for example: "If a man is, an animal is." Whereby it must be noted that one thing follows from another in many ways because certain things follow from the essentially superior, as *differentia,* genus, and definition follow from species. Another case is that of an essential part from a whole; for example, body and soul from man. Another example is that of an integral part, just as the head and the foot from a whole man or a wall, a roof, and a foundation from a house. Another example is that of proper accidents from a subject; as from a man, risible. Another case is that of an extrinsic cause from an effect; as for example, a chariot follows from a horse. Another type is that of an effect from a cause; for example, the generation of living things follows from the sun's approaching us. Another kind is that of a relative from a correlative, for example, from half, double; and from antecedence, consecution—for they are called correlatives. The division of these types can be seen particularly in dialectical proofs. But this conjunction "if" is indifferently related to any type whatever of consecution. This division of consequences is taken from the point of view of the relation of things or from the point of view of the matter. But the divisions are taken from the point of view of the mode of arguing.

The first of these is that of consecutions. Another is that of simultaneous existents in time, as for example: "If a man is, an animal is." Another is that of prior and posterior existents in time, which happens in two ways. In one way the prior in time follows from the posterior, as "If bread is, water and flour were." And this always happens in the case of non-permanent causes, as in the case of those things whose cause precedes its effect chronologically and naturally. In another way the posterior in time follows from the prior, as for example, "If cleansing and every requisite for health exists, health will exist." This happens in the case of the final cause which is sometimes posterior in time to its effect, although it is naturally prior. From this it is clear that the prior sometimes follows in the present, sometimes in the past, and sometimes in the future. Accordingly a cause is related in three ways to its effect. For sometimes the cause is simultaneous in time with its effect, although it is naturally posterior, for example, the soul and a man. Sometimes the cause precedes the effect in time, as fire, smoke; a cluster of grapes, wine. Sometimes indeed the cause is posterior in time but naturally prior to its effect, as in the case of a final cause which can be acquired through movement on the part of its subject.

The second division is of consequences: one is simple; the other is composite. A simple consequence is one which consists of a simple antecedent and a simple consequent, as "Man is; therefore animal is." A composite consequence is one in which many inferences are made. And this is twofold, because one is the consequence in itself, the other is the opposite consequence. The consequence in itself follows when it is indicated that the opposite of the consequent follows from the opposite of the antecedent. And it holds in the case of relative opposites, as: "If double is, the multiple is; therefore if less than double is, less than the multiple is"; and in the case of contraries, as: "If virtue is, good is; therefore if vice is, evil is"; and in the case of privative opposites, as: "If sight is, sensibility is; therefore if blindness is, insensibility is." But it does not hold in the case of contradictory opposites, because one would be arguing from the destruction of the antecedent to the destruction of the consequent—as was seen in the case of the fallacy of the consequent. The other is that which follows when the opposite of the antecedent is inferred from the opposite of the consequent. And this holds with contradictories, as for example: "If a man is, an animal is; therefore if no animal is, no man is." But it does not hold in the case of the other opposites, except perhaps on account of the matter. And these consequences can be fashioned indifferently in the form of one consequence or in the form of many. In one, as: "Every virtue is good; therefore every vice is bad"; and in many, as was seen previously. These two divisions of consequences are related to each other as the exceeding and the exceeded. For each member of the first division can be divided by the second division, and in this way the first can be regarded as the exceeding; similarly each member of the second division can be divided by the first division, and thus the first is regarded as the exceeded.

With regard to what has been said, this sophism is discussed: "If no time is, some time is." *The proof:* If no time is, day is not—by a topical argument from a quantitative whole. But if day is not, night is—from immediate contradictories. But if night is, some time is. Therefore from the first to the last: "If no time is, some time is."

To the contrary: In this case an opposite is signified to follow from an opposite. Therefore, the statement is false and impossible.

Solution: The initial statement is false and the disproof holds. Regarding the proof we say that the second consequence, namely, "If day is not, night is," holds in one way but not in another. For in "Day is not," the negation, taken generically, can be in one way [the one] which negates the form and leaves a subject, but the negation of a subject or a privative negation is affirmed in another way. But in this way one posits the existence of time which is common to day and night. And in this way it validly follows that "Day is not; therefore night is." But one does not understand that "day is not" in this way in the first consequence. In another way the negation can be outside the genus, one which is said to be a negation negating and leaving nothing. And in this way the first consequence holds, when one says: "If no time is, day is not"; but the second does not hold, when one says: "If day is not, night is," because a topical argument from immediate contraries does not hold destructively except with a constant subject. But then one ought to argue as follows: "Time is; but day is not; therefore night is."

With regard to what has been said, this sophism is discussed: "If no proposition is true, some proposition is true." *The proof:* If no proposition is true, this proposition: "Man is not," is not true—from a quantitative whole. But if this: "Man is not," is not true, its contradictory is true—from contradictory opposition. But if its contradictory is true, some proposition is true. Therefore from the first to the last: "If no proposition is true, some proposition is true."

To the contrary: In this case an opposite follows from an opposite. Therefore the statement is impossible.

Solution: The initial statement is ambiguous. For in the proposition: "No proposition is true," the negation can be taken absolutely and outside of the genus. But then it removes both the proposition and its truth. Thus it does not follow that "No proposition is true; therefore this proposition: 'Man is not,' is not true." Nor is there in this case a topical argument from a quantitative whole, because in this way the antecedent posits nothing, neither the proposition nor its truth. But the consequent posits the proposition with the value of a demonstration, as when one says: "This proposition: 'Man is not,' is not true." But in this way the consequent of the initial proposition contradicts the antecedent. Therefore in this way the initial statement is false and also the proof. In the other way the negation can be taken generically. In this way no proposition is true. It posits every proposition and removes every truth from the proposition. Taken thus, the sophism is true because its antecedent posits all contradictories to be simultaneously false. Hence in regard to the consequent it posits all contradictories to be simultaneously true, because whenever one contradictory is false, the other is true. Therefore the initial statement is true and it is one conditional whose consequent necessarily follows from the antecedent. As to the disproof, one must say that in this case an opposite does not follow from an opposite but rather one part of a contradiction follows from an antecedent which includes in itself every contradiction whatever.

With regard to what has been said, this sophism is discussed: "If you are everywhere, you are not everywhere." *The proof:* If you are everywhere, you are here. And if you are here, you are not there. But if you are not there, you are not everywhere. Therefore from the first to the last: "If you are everywhere, you are not everywhere."

To the contrary: In this case an opposite follows from an opposite. Therefore the statement is impossible.

Solution: The initial statement is absolutely true, because it is one conditional in which the consequent necessarily follows from the antecedent by virtue of the fact that the first antecedent, namely, "You are everywhere," posits a contradiction from the point of view of the subject and from the point of view of its predicate. The pronoun "you," posited in the subject, denotes a singular thing fitted by nature to be only in one place. Therefore from the point of view of the subject it posits that "You are not everywhere." But from the point of view of the predicate it posits that "You are everywhere." Thus it posits a contradiction and not only one contradiction but rather several, because, just as it is impossible that many bodies be circumscriptively in one place, so it is impossible for the same body to be in different places circumscriptively. Whence because it is here circumscriptively, it is neither there nor there and so on with regard to any other particular place whatever. Therefore "to be everywhere" posits as many contradictions in relation to "to be here" as there are particular places different from this place. Hence when one says "You are everywhere," several contradictions, of which one part is posited in the consequent, are asserted. To the disproof, one answers that an opposite does not follow from an opposite but rather one part of a contradiction follows from an antecedent which includes each part.

Having discussed consecutive words, we must consider the mode of syllogizing with conditionals. For, with regard to syllogisms, one type is a categorical; another type is a hypothetical which is constructed of conditional propositions. Therefore, a conditional proposition is capable of being syllogized. And it is necessary in this case that a descent be made under the antecedent or under the consequent. Hence, as a consequence, we must see how the descent happens sometimes under the antecedent and sometimes under the consequent, and in this regard many rules are given.

The first is: If general terms are posited in the antecedent, a descent can be made under them, the consequent remaining unchanged; for example: "If a man runs, an animal runs. Therefore if Plato runs, an animal runs; and if Sortes runs, an animal runs—and so on."

The second rule is: If general terms are posited distributively in the antecedent and in the consequent, the antecedent remains unchanged and a descent can be made under the consequent; for example: "If every animal runs, every man runs. Therefore if every animal runs, Sortes runs and Plato runs and so on."

The third rule is: If any one thing follows from another, the consequent being destroyed, the antecedent is destroyed. Hence an affirmation from the destruction of the consequent to the destruction of the antecedent is valid; for example: "If it is a man, it is an animal. Therefore if it is not an animal, it is not a man."

The fourth rule: If one thing follows from another, the antecedent having been posited, the consequent is posited. Hence, an affirmation from the positing of the antecedent to the positing of the consequent is valid; for example: "If the sun shines, it is day."

The fifth rule: Whatever is antecedent to the antecedent, is antecedent to the consequent; for example: "If an animal is, a substance is. But if a man is, an animal is. Therefore if a man is, a substance is."

The sixth rule: Whatever follows from the consequent, follows from the antecedent; for example: "If a man is, an animal is. And if an animal is, a substance is. Therefore if a man is, a substance is." On account of this rule a consequence from the first to the last is valid, which is to say that whenever many consequences are posited, then that which is the consequent in the first becomes the antecedent of the second and the last consequent is denoted as following from the first antecedent.

But in order to see negation and contradiction in modal propositions and in conditional propositions, this rule is posited: In the case of a negative conditional, neither its antecedent nor its consequent ought to be negated absolutely, but rather the consequence of the consequent from the antecedent. The reason is that the conditional does not posit its antecedent nor its consequent absolutely but rather the relationship of the antecedent to the consequent. Hence, this is negative: "It is not the case that if Sortes runs, a man is moved," but not this: "If a man runs, a man is not moved," for in the case of the second proposition the relationship of the antecedent to the consequent which is signified by that conjunction "if" is denied. From this it is clear that to cause a contradiction of any conditional, it is necessary to deny that the consequent follows from the antecedent or to posit beforehand a negation of the whole conditional; for example, these are contradictory: "If a man is, an animal is" and "*It is not the case that if a man is, an animal is.*" Hence there is the rule: Whenever a negation is posited before any categorical or conditional proposition, it produces the contradictory. Therefore it is said that it is no more true to cite the contradiction than to posit a negation before the whole proposition. Secondly, it follows that the truth of a conditional is caused by the relationship of the antecedent to the consequent and not from the connection of the predicate with the subject, neither in the antecedent nor in the consequent, as it is caused in categoricals. Wherefore, every true conditional is necessary and every false conditional is impossible. For a relationship of such a kind when it is true is necessary and when it is false is impossible, because it is founded on universal intentions, as are "whole," "part," "genus," and such like, which are always necessary or impossible. Further it follows that from the impossible not anything whatever follows. The reason is that in the case of every consequence the antecedent is the cause of the consequent, either as the cause of the being or at least as the cause of the following from another, only if it enjoys in itself the relationship of including or containing; but the impossible cannot have such a relationship to anything; therefore, anything does not follow from the impossible. Hence an impossible composition can be considered in three ways: in one way as impossible; in another way as composition; in a third way as a composition of things which are arranged in a statement or in an argumentation. In the first two ways, absolutely nothing follows from the impossible because in that way a consideration of the relationship of containing cannot exist. But in the third way anything follows from the impossible; sometimes on account of a relationship of the things from which an impossible composition arises, as "If a stone is, a man is an animal"; at other times, on account of the arrangement of the form of arguing, as for example, in the case of "Every stone is an animal; a tree is a stone; therefore a tree is an animal," the conclusion follows by virtue of the form of arguing and not on account of the impossibility of the premises. For the same reason it is held that the necessary does not follow from anything whatever by virtue of the fact that the necessary cannot enjoy the relationship of containing with regard to any consequent whatever of anything.

From what has been said, the falsity of two rules held by the ancients is obvious. The first [rule] is: "From the impossible anything follows," so that every conditional would be true whose antecedent will have been impossible; for example: "If Plato is an ass, Plato is a stone." The second rule [is] that "The necessary follows from anything whatever," on which account every conditional is said to be true whose consequent is necessary, no matter what the antecedent will have been; for example: "If Plato is a stone, a man is an animal," was said to be necessary because for the truth of a conditional it is required that the antecedent cannot be true without the consequent being true. Nay, rather when the antecedent in a conditional is impossible, although it can in no way be true without the consequent being true, and when the consequent is necessary, the conditional is always true; therefore the antecedent cannot be true without the consequent being true; consequently, such conditionals are said to be true. But, as has been said, anything whatever does not follow from the impossible, nor does the necessary follow from anything whatever. Therefore those rules are false. With regard to their reasoning it is said that it does not suffice for the truth of a conditional that the antecedent as such cannot be true, but rather it is required that it cannot be true without including the truth of the consequent. Therefore in this case negation denies the separation of the truth of the consequent from the truth of the antecedent.

With regard to what has been said, this sophism is discussed: "If nothing is, something is." *The proof:* If nothing is, nothing is is true. But if nothing is is true, the assertible "Nothing is" is true—by a topical argument from the convertible. But if this assertible is true, something is is true—from a subjective part. But if something is is true, "Something is"—from the convertible, because to be and to be true are convertible. Therefore from the first to the last: "If nothing is, something is."

To the contrary: In this case it is denoted that an opposite follows from an opposite. Therefore the statement is impossible.

Solution: The initial statement is false, namely, "If nothing is, something is," as the disproof proves. As to the proof, one answers that the first consequence is valid when one says: "If nothing is, nothing is is true," because from the impossible the impossible follows as long as there shall have been some relation to itself and then there is a causal topical argument from an assertible truth. The second consequence also holds, namely, "Nothing is is true; therefore this assertible 'Nothing is' is true." But the third consequence errs in passing from a relative statement to an absolute statement, namely, "If this assertible is true etc.," because "assertible" cannot be something absolutely but only relatively and the term "something" posits being in the absolute. Therefore in this case one is arguing from the relative to the absolute. Also when it is said: "If this assertible is true, something is is true," the assertible "Nothing is" is signified by the pronoun "this," because "nothing" denotes non-being. But the essence is removed by the consequent, "something is *(esse)* is true"— "is" *(esse)* is posited absolutely and so it posits being absolutely. Hence if anyone will have correctly examined the third conditional, he will see that its consequent contradicts the cause. Therefore "nothing" posits nothing manifest in this case, or, if it does, it falls into the fallacy of relative to absolute.

With regard to what has been said, the following sophism is discussed: "Sortes speaks the truth, if only Plato is speaking." Let it be posited that Sortes says that only Plato is speaking. *The proof:* Sortes says that only Plato is speaking. This is true, if only Plato is speaking. Therefore "Sortes speaks the truth, if only Plato is speaking."

To the contrary: If only Plato is speaking, no one other than Plato is speaking—from the described or from the defined. And if no one other than Plato is speaking, Sortes is not speaking—from a quantitative whole. But if Sortes is not speaking, Sortes does not speak the truth —by an argument from the genus, because "to speak" is superior to "to speak the truth" and "to speak the false." Therefore it does not follow that: "Sortes speaks the truth, if only Plato is speaking."

Solution: The initial statement is false and it posits a contradiction, because it posits "only Plato" and "not only Plato" to speak when it posits that Sortes "speaks the truth," and "does not speak the truth" since all others than Plato are excluded with respect to that act of speaking. The proof errs by the fallacy of accident, because, although "only Plato is speaking" may be true by itself, if only Plato is speaking, nevertheless it cannot be true with this added: "Sortes speaks the truth," because Sortes is excluded from the act of speaking. Therefore it is a fallacy of accident. Just as if Coruscus himself were known and that he be busy, nevertheless it does not follow that a busy [person] is known. Nay, rather in that case there is a fallacy of accident.

With regard to what has been said, this sophism is discussed: "If you know that you are a stone, you do not know that you are a stone." *The proof:* If "You know that you are a stone" is true—because nothing is known except the truth—then, if "You know that you are a stone" is true, "You are a stone"—from the convertible, since the statement is convertible with the proposition. But if you are a stone, you know nothing—by an argument from opposites. But if you know nothing, you do not know that you are a stone—from a quantitative whole. Therefore from the first to the last: "If you know that you are a stone, you do not know that you are a stone."

To the contrary: In this case an opposite follows from an opposite. Therefore, etc.

Solution: The sophism is true because the consequent necessarily follows from the antecedent, as is obvious. To the disproof one answers that in this case an opposite does not follow from an opposite but rather one part of a contradiction follows from the antecedent which includes each of the two parts within itself. For the antecedent: "You know that you are a stone," by virtue of the verb "you know" posits knowledge in the subject from the point of view of the object of knowledge, but "you are a stone" deprives the subject of knowledge, therefore it posits the subject "knows" and "does not know," "is a stone" and "is not a stone," and "does not know that it is a stone." Therefore, from the first antecedent, which includes all these contradictions, the consequent follows, not on account of from the impossible anything follows, but rather because from an integral whole any part of it follows.

Having spoken of consecutive words, we must speak of the verbs

[58]

"begins" (*incipit*) and "ends" (*desinit*), which are called syncategorematic words because affirmation and negation are understood in their exposition and because their signification is varied by the adjuncts. For according as they are attributed to permanent or successive things, they are expounded sometimes in one way and sometimes in another, because their signification depends on these things. Hence such verbs as "begins" and "ends" signify the inceptions or cessations of mutable things or they signify the being or non-being of things in their initial and final boundaries. For "begins" signifies the inception which is the beginning of the being or non-being of a thing. Thus it denotes being with a terminus. "Ends" signifies the cessation which is the term of the being or non-being of a thing. And they logically follow each other reciprocally, for what begins to be, ceases to not be; and what ceases to be, begins to not be. Both, therefore, refer to the same thing indivisibly: for example, when something begins to be a man, it ceases to not be a man; and when something ceases to not be a man, it begins to be a man. But because the signification of these words is varied with different things, therefore to see their signification in the particular, we must first of all consider things.

Certainly as far as things are concerned, some are permanent, others successive. Things are called permanent whose whole beings exist simultaneously and not one part after another, as are a man, wood, a stone. Indeed, things are called successive whose beings are not simultaneously whole but rather according to the prior and the posterior, so that one part succeeds another, for example, motion, an action, time. But there are two *differentiae* of these things. The first is that the being of permanent things is a simultaneous whole, but the being of successive things is not a simultaneous whole, nay rather it exists only in the case of a succession of parts. The second *differentia* is: the parts of permanent things can exist simultaneously, as a part of a man or a stone; but the parts of successive things cannot exist simultaneously, for example, two parts of the same motion cannot exist simultaneously, nor two parts of time, but rather one exists after another successively—it is impossible for many things to exist simultaneously. A third *differentia* is: permanent things are prior by nature, while successive things are posterior, because permanent things are the cause of successive things. A fourth *differentia* is: permanent things are terminated in themselves but successive things are not terminated in themselves, rather they are terminated in permanent things, as, for example, motion in a quantity or a quality.

Likewise, with regard to permanent things, some are acquired indivisibly, as the light of day in the air and such like; others, indeed, [are acquired] in time, through intension or through extension, as those things whose being is divisible according to the parts of the intension, as whiteness or blackness, or according to the parts of the extension, as length, width. Hence in the case of permanent things whose being is acquired indivisibly, it is possible to give the first instant of its being and of its non-being but the ultimate instant of its non-being with regard to the part before is not given, nor of its being with regard to the part after; for example, the first instant of the being of a man, a horse, a bicubital, a tricubital is given, but the ultimate instant of its non-being is not given, nor of its being. But in the case of successive and permanent things whose being is not acquired instantly, the first instant of its being is not given nor the ultimate instant, as, for example, motion or time, but the ultimate instant of its non-being with respect to the part before is given and the first instant of its non-being with respect to the part after. For while they have being at some time, they enjoy non-being at the terminus of that time; and just as there is no intermediate between a time and its terminus, so neither is there between its being and its non-being. From this it is clear that absolutely permanent things enjoy being in relation to their beginning and non-being in relation to their end, since in their case the first instant but not the ultimate instant of their being can be given. But successive things, since they do not have either a first or an ultimate instant of their genus—for the beginning or end of time is not time but an instant, nor is the terminus of motion motion but rather a change—therefore do not have being in their beginning nor in their end. Since the verb "begins" affirms the beginning of the being of a thing, it therefore has a different signification with respect to permanent things and with respect to successive things, for which reason some rules are stated.

The first rule is: The verb "begins" when it is connected with permanent things whose being is acquired indivisibly, affirms a positing of the present and a negation of the past, as, for example, when one says: "Plato begins to be a man," that is, "Plato now is a man but previously he was not a man."

Another rule is that the verb "begins" when it is connected with successive things and with permanent things whose being is not acquired instantly, affirms a negation of the present and a positing of the future by virtue of the fact that successive things do not possess being at their beginning: for example, when one says: "Motion begins being," the meaning is: "Motion now is not but immediately after this it will be"; or "Sortes begins to be white," because something is only said to be white through an excess of white over black which is acquired through motion. And the approach is not made through the indivisible but through the divisible, but not the infinite. Therefore the first instant in which something can be said to be white cannot be given except by speaking of the perfect being of the white which is acquired at the terminus of the movement. Therefore the meaning of that is: "Sortes now is not white but immediately after this he will be white." Similarly here: "Sortes begins being equal to Plato," the meaning is: "Sortes now is not equal to Plato but immediately after this he will be equal to Plato." But being equal is formed of the indivisible, therefore "begins" taken with this name "equal" ought to be expounded in the same manner as with the other permanent things whose being is acquired in an instant.

Another rule is: The verb "ends" connected with everything when it is added to being itself, affirms the negation of the present and the positing of the past. The reason is that the ultimate instant of the being of the thing is not given, both in the case of permanent things and in the case of successive things: for example, when one says: "Plato ceases to be a man," the meaning is: "Plato now is not a man but immediately prior to this he was a man," or "Plato now at last was a man"; and when one says: "Motion ceases to exist," the meaning is: "Motion now is not but immediately prior to this it was." Similarly, when the verb "ceases" is added to the non-being of absolutely permanent things, it affirms the negation of the present and the positing of the past; for example, when one says: "The matter of water ceases not being air," the meaning is: "The matter of water is not now contained under the non-being of air but immediately before this it was contained under that non-being." But when "ceases" is added to the non-being of successive things, it affirms the positing of the present and the negation of the future, because the ultimate instant of the non-being of successive things is given; for example, when one says: "Plato ceases being in motion," the meaning is: "Plato now is not in motion but immediately after this he will not have non-being in motion."

From what has been said, it is clear that verbs of this kind, namely, "begins" and "ceases," cause us to understand different times with respect to that which is signified by them. They do not, however, signify these different times equally in the beginning but rather according to the prior and the posterior. The reason is that they always assert the affirmation of one time and the negation of another, and they consignify the being of a thing along with a termination. They always affirm primarily that time of which they assert the affirmation rather than that time of which they assert the negation, because affirmation pertains to the being of a thing, but negation pertains to the non-being of a thing. If it be said that they affirm the being at different times, since they always imply different times, it must be said that time can be taken in two ways. In one way, properly, as it is a measure of motion. And it is implied in this way regarding that which is signified by those verbs. But the verb is not asserted of any time on the basis of that time. In another way, it is taken as affirming a mode of being in time. But thus it is a mode of signifying. And on this basis the verb is asserted of any time. Therefore this verb "begins," from the point of view of that mode of signifying, refers only to present time, although it implies different times from the point of view of that which is signified by it.

With regard to what has been said, the following sophism is discussed: "Sortes ceases to be the whitest of men." Let it be assumed that Sortes always will have been the whitest of men but now one whiter than he is born. *The proof:* Sortes now is not the whitest of men but immediately prior to this he was the whitest of men. Therefore the initial statement is true.

To the contrary: Sortes ceases being the whitest of men. Either therefore of the men who are, or of the men who are not, or of the men of whom some are and some are not, each of which is false.

Solution: The initial statement is true and the proof holds. But the disproof errs according to the fallacy of accident because the cessation or the "cease being the whitest" in the initial statement signifies with reference to men taken absolutely in general but not with reference to the men who are or the men who are not taken particularly. Whence it is not necessary if something is proper to something in relation to something superior, that therefore it is proper to it in relation to its inferiors; rather in such cases a fallacy of accident is committed.

This sophism is discussed: "Sortes ceases knowing everything he knew." Let it be posited that Sortes always knew three assertibles which are designated "a," "b," "c"; and let "d" be a fourth of which he now loses knowledge. *The proof:* Sortes knows not now everything that he knew. But immediately prior to this he knew everything that he knew. Therefore "Sortes ceases knowing, etc."

To the contrary: Sortes ceases knowing everything he knew. But Sortes knew "a." Therefore he ceases to know "a."

Solution: The initial statement is false as is clear from the disproof. As to the proof one answers that the major premise is ambiguous, namely, "Sortes knows not now everything that he knew," by virtue of the fact that the negation can precede the distribution; and then it [i.e., the major] is true, because, posited that Sortes does not know that assertible "d," in that way the conclusion does not follow; in another way the negation can follow the distribution and the meaning is: "Everything Sortes knew, he now knows," but in this way it is false and the conclusion follows. Whereby this rule must be noted: Whenever "begins" or "ceases" is connected with a multitude or with a plural noun, they ought to be expounded by removing the multitude as a whole or each one of the multitude; for example, in the case of: "Sortes ceases knowing everything that he knew," the meaning is: "Everything Sortes knew, he does not know now but immediately prior to this he knew," and similarly of the others.

This sophism is discussed: "Sortes ceases to know that he ceases to know nothing." Let it be posited that Sortes knows three assertibles necessarily, so that he never forgets, namely, "a," "b," "c"; and that along with these he shall have known the assertible "he ceases to know nothing," but now he forgets this. *The proof:* Sortes does not know now that he ceases to know nothing. But immediately prior to this he knew. Therefore "Sortes ceases to know that he ceases to know nothing."

To the contrary: Sortes ceases to know that he ceases to know nothing. Therefore he knew that "he ceases to know nothing." But whatever is known is necessary. Therefore that "Sortes ceases to know nothing" is necessary. Therefore "he ceases to know nothing." And consequently, he does not cease to know the assertible: "he ceases to know nothing."

Solution: The initial statement is true and the proof holds. But the disproof errs by reasoning fallaciously from the relative to the absolute, in inferring as follows: "Sortes ceases to know nothing. Therefore, he does not cease to know the assertible: 'he ceases to know nothing.'" For to know this assertible or another is not possible except that he knows the other three assertibles. But for him to know those three assertibles is to know only by reflection; but it does not increase knowledge and at the same time it does not lessen knowledge. Just as if someone were to see a colored object and he were to see that he saw a colored object, he does not see more than by seeing the colored object only. Therefore one is arguing from the relative to the absolute when one infers that: "He ceases to know nothing; therefore he does not cease to know that 'he ceases to know nothing.'"

With regard to the supposition of terms used with the aforementioned verbs, here are some rules. The first is: General terms following the verbs "begins" and "ends" have a dual supposition. The reason is that these verbs posit an affirmation and a negation. Certainly, in the affirmation the terms can have determinate and simple supposition; but in the negation, confused supposition: for example, when one says: "Sortes begins being a man," the meaning is: "Now he is a man but prior to this he was not a man"; in the first proposition "man" denotes simply, but in the second, distributively.

[63]

The second rule is: In the case of the verbs "begins" and "ends" an argument from the inferior to the superior is not valid, nor contrariwise from the point of view of the predicate. This is because of the affirmation and the negation which they imply in their exposition. For on account of the affirmation an argument from the superior to the inferior is not valid; but on account of the negation a converse argument is not valid. Just as it does not follow that: "Sortes begins being bicubital; therefore he begins being a quantum"; and conversely it does not follow: "Sortes begins being a quantum; therefore he begins being bicubital." Rather a fallacy of the consequent is committed in both ways, as was stated. And "from the point of view of the predicate" was stated expressly, because from the point of view of the subject, such verbs do not have supposition. Therefore one can argue validly from the inferior to the superior in the case of the affirmative or contrariwise in the case of the negative; for example: "A man begins being moved; therefore an animal begins being moved" or "No animal begins running; therefore neither does a man."

With regard to what has been said, this sophism is discussed: "Sortes ceases being not ceasing being." Let it be posited that Sortes is at the moment of death. *The proof:* Sortes is not not ceasing being. But immediately prior he was not ceasing being. Therefore "he ceases being not ceasing being."

To the contrary: Sortes ceases being not ceasing being. Therefore Sortes ceases being while he does not cease being, or if he does not cease being, or because he does not cease being. For a gerund ending in "-ing" has to be resolved by "while" *(dum)*, by "if" *(si)*, or by "because" *(quia)*, just as a posited ablative absolute. But each of these is false. Therefore the sophism also is false.

Solution: The initial statement is ambiguous by virtue of the fact that the determination "not ceasing being" can determine the verb "ceases" or the verb "being." If it determines the verb "ceases," then it is false, because opposites are simultaneously posited of the same thing, namely, cessation and the privation of cessation. But in this way the disproof holds. If, however, it determines the verb "being," then it would be true, because the meaning is that "Sortes ceases being not ceasing being" or "He ceases to have unceasing being." Hence although he does not cease being, nevertheless he ceases being absolutely such, namely, unceasing or without cessation, because *de cetero* he does not have such being as such but rather he has ceasing being. In the first way it is composite and false. In the second way it is divided and true. Hence in this case there is a fallacy of composition. Furthermore, there is the rule: Whenever verbs of this sort, namely, "begins" and "ceases," are added to a term implying in itself a subject (or individual) and an accident, or a substance and an accidental form, the statement is ambiguous by virtue of the fact that the beginning or ceasing can be signified with respect to the subject or with respect to the accident; for example, "Plato begins being white" can be understood as either that "he begins being" absolutely, or that "he begins being white," which is accidental.

This sophism is discussed: "Plato begins being another of these." Let it be posited that Plato will have been previously while Sortes begins being newly. *The proof:* Plato is another of these. But previously he was not another of them. Therefore, the sophism is true.

To the contrary: Plato begins being another of them. Therefore either Plato or Sortes begins being, because no one is another of them except Sortes and Plato. But Plato does not begin being, because Plato was previously; nor does Sortes begin being, because they are distinct. Therefore the initial statement is false.

Solution: The initial statement is ambiguous by virtue of the fact that there are two things understood in the term "another," namely, a subject denoted in which there is an accident and the accident itself which is the otherness. Therefore the beginning which refers to the being able to be "another" can be denied relative to the subject denoted or relative to the accident. If relative to the subject denoted, then it is false and the disproof holds because the meaning is: "Plato begins being another of these," that is, "begins being Plato or Sortes." If relative to the accident, then it is true as proven, and the meaning is: "Plato begins being another of them," that is, "begins being under the otherness of them." Although Plato's being does not begin absolutely, nevertheless it begins being under the otherness. In this way there is a fallacy of accident in the disproof. But in the first way the disproof holds. Hence, universally in the case of any good distinction whatever solving sophisms, in the sense in which it is conceded to be true, the proof is true and the disproof is in error, and contrariwise; also it is always true in one sense but false in the other.

Having considered the verbs "begins" and "ceases," we must as a consequence treat of the words "necessarily" and "contingently." In the first place we must see what the necessary may be and in how many ways it is spoken of and how it varies the meaning of a proposition.

That is called necessary being which is impossible to be otherwise and is impossible to be changed, because to be changed is to be otherwise now than before. Therefore it is impossible for the necessary to be changed. But being impossible to be changed is always being. Therefore the necessary is that which is always being. And thus it is sempiternal or eternal. Hence the necessary includes being as subject or material cause, and immutability as formal cause.

But the necessary is spoken of in two ways. For something is said to be absolutely necessary, as God's existence is absolutely necessary. In another way the necessary is spoken of with respect to the supposition of something, and then it is spoken of relatively; for example, it is necessary for a man to have a ship, not absolutely but on the supposition that he is obliged by circumstances to sail. But this necessity arises from the point of view of the final cause, which is a cause posterior to its own effect in the order of being although not in the order of causation. But absolute necessity in the case of created things arises from the other causes which are prior, and there are three modes of it in accordance with the other three causes. In the first way something is necessary from the point of view of the efficient cause, either from natural necessity, as it is necessary for the warmed earth to be dessicated, or from violent necessity, as it is necessary for a struck curtain to be moved. In another way something is necessary from the point of view of the matter, as it is necessary that a mixture composed of contraries be corrupted. In another way, something is necessary from the point of view of form, as it is necessary that a being having a rational soul be a man. In all of these ways the necessary is impossible to be otherwise in any way, either absolutely or from the point of view of supposition.

Moreover such necessity is a certain mode of being which is related as a determination of that to which it is added. And it can determine three things in order, namely, the composition of the proposition, the composition of the concepts of the intellect, and the being which is in reality, insofar as these three are related in order, as the sign, the signified, and the determinable unity. For the proposition signifies the composition which exists in the intellect, and the composition of the intellect signifies the being which is in reality; for example, in saying: "Man is necessarily an animal," one signifies that this "Every man is an animal" is necessary, also the necessity of the composition which exists in the intellect, and [that] that which it is to be an animal necessarily is in man. And the necessary can sometimes affirm the necessary relationship of the predicate to the subject; and thus it affirms the necessity of the consequent, as: "That man is an animal is necessary." In fact, [the necessary] sometimes affirms the necessary relationship of the antecedent to the consequent, for example, "It is necessary that a man be moved, if he runs," and thus it affirms the necessity of the consequent. And each mode of necessity can in one way be the object of attention among determinate things and then it pertains to demonstrative science. In another way [each

[66]

mode of necessity can be the object of attention] among universal intentions and then it pertains to dialectic, as, for example, when one says: "A man is risible; therefore an animal is risible." Or the necessity of the consequence from the relationship of those determinate things can be the object of attention as, evidently, animal is included in man; and then it pertains to physics. In another way from the universal relationship of intentions, namely, of a species in relation to a genus, by virtue of which everything which is predicated of a species, is also predicated of a genus; and then it causes a dialectical syllogism. Nevertheless it is the same necessity which is explained in discourse in each way. But it is expounded in the first way determinately and in the second way confusedly, because the relation of species to genus is found not only between man and animal but also in the case of many others. Nevertheless "the necessary" (*necessarium*) and "necessary" (*necesse*) and "necessarily" (*necessario*) differ. For "the necessary" affirms immutability nominally. Therefore it is a nominal mode and it determines composition taken nominally. But the others affirm immutability taken verbally. These in turn differ, because "necessary" is added universally to the verb "is," as, for example, "It is necessary that Sortes run"; but the other form is added to other verbs, as, for example, "Sortes runs necessarily."

We now discuss the word "contingent." The contingent, generally speaking, is said to be everything which is possible being. In this way it is converted with the possible. And it is divided into the necessary contingent and the non-necessary. The necessary contingent is that which is and cannot not be, as, for example, man's being an animal; of this one must speak just as one speaks of the necessary. But the contingent in relation to whichever of the two you please is that which can be and not be, as for a man to sit, an animal to run. And such is said to be contingent in relation to whichever of the two you please by virtue of the fact that it is related to each of the opposites. This is again divided into the natural contingent, the rare contingent, and the indefinite contingent. The natural contingent is that which is more able to be than not to be, as for example, for a man to become gray in old age. And it is called natural contingent because it has a natural relationship to being. But the rare contingent is that which is more able not to be than to be, as, for example, for a man to become gray in youth. This is called rare because it rarely happens. The indefinite contingent is that which is equally able to be and not to be, as, for example, for a man to run tomorrow. And it is called indefinite because it is not determined to either part of the contradiction but is determined to one by its cause. And sometimes contingent is affirmed in relation to whichever of two you please, properly speaking, because it is related equally to whichever of the two you please of contradictories, namely, in relation to being and to non-being. This division, however, is not a division of a genus into its species but of an analogy into its analogates, because, divided according to what is prior and what is posterior, it is affirmed of the dividing members. And one must speak in the same way of the preceding divisions.

Regarding what has been said, this sophism is considered: "Every man of necessity is an animal." *The proof:* The proposition "Man is an animal," is true. Therefore the proposition itself modified by a mode of necessity will be true. Therefore the proposition itself is true.

To the contrary: Every man necessarily is an animal. Sortes is a man. Therefore Sortes necessarily is an animal. Therefore Sortes necessarily is. But this is false. Therefore that from which it follows [is false].

Solution: The initial proposition is absolutely true. As to the disproof one answers that in that case there is a fallacy of reasoning from the relative to the absolute. For when one says: "Sortes necessarily is an animal," essential being, which is being relatively, is predicated; but when one says: "Sortes of necessity is," actual being, which is being absolutely with respect to that same essential being, is predicated.

This sophism is considered: "The soul of the antichrist necessarily will be." *The proof:* The soul of the antichrist will be, assuming that he will be in time. But whenever he will be, it necessarily will be. Therefore the initial proposition is true.

To the contrary: The soul of the antichrist necessarily will be. Therefore, that the soul of the antichrist be, is necessary. But this is false, since that the antichrist be is contingent, therefore also his soul.

Solution: The initial proposition is false and the disproof holds. But the proof errs in reasoning from the relative to the absolute. For when one says: "The soul of the antichrist, whenever it will be, will be necessarily," necessity is there posited on the supposition that it is a relative necessity; but when one infers: "Therefore the soul of the antichrist will be necessarily," absolute necessity is posited and absolutely. Hence the conclusion does not follow. Just as it does not follow: "Sortes while he sits, necessarily sits. Therefore Sortes necessarily sits," rather one is arguing from the relative to the absolute. If, however, the term "necessarily" in the sophism were to affirm necessity from the point of view of supposition in such a way that the sense were: "The soul of the antichrist while it will be, necessarily will be," the sophism could be true. And because every analogue, posited by itself, is taken for its more principal significate, therefore "necessarily" in this case affirms necessity absolutely. Similarly if "necessarily" were to determine the predicate as such so that the sense would be: "The soul of the antichrist will be necessarily," that is, "will be a necessary being," the sophism could be true. However, because "necessarily" from the meaning of the word has to determine the composition but not the predicate as such, we should not take that sense into consideration. But in order to see how such words determine the composition of a proposition, some rules are given.

The first is: "Contingent" and "possible" amplify the composition of a proposition to the present and the future. The reason is that each of these affirms composition and potency or possibility, which potency is extended to the present and the future but not to the past, because in relation to the past there is no potency. From this rule it follows that "contingent" and "possible" amplify the subject of a proposition to stand for present and future subjects due to the fact that, the composition having been amplified, the extremes of the composition are amplified likewise. Since words of this kind amplify composition relative to the present and relative to the future, they therefore amplify the subject, if it can be amplified, to stand for present and future subjects.

The second rule is: "Necessary" amplifies the composition to all time affirmatively, and "impossible" to all time negatively. The reason is that "the necessary" is said to be that which is always being and "the impossible" that which is always non-being. Now all time is signified by what is affirmed, namely, "always." Therefore, when "always being" is affirmed, all time is posited affirmatively; and when this is said, "always non-being," all time is posited negatively. From this it follows that "necessary" and "impossible" amplify the extremes of a composition to stand for all time. Consequently they amplify to the subjects of any time whatever due to the fact that they amplify in relation to the composition. Similarly they amplify the extremes of a composition; as when one says: "Every man necessarily is an animal," "man" and "animal" are amplified in this case to the present, the past, and the future.

It follows from these rules that "contingent," "necessary," and "impossible" differ and amplify the composition of a proposition in different ways. For "contingent" amplifies by way of the potentiality and the imperfection which it signifies. On the other hand, "necessary" amplifies by way of the actuality which it affirms, insofar as it is always being. And "impossible" amplifies by way of the privation of the potentiality and even of the actuality which it signifies. For "impossible" primarily negates potency; but secondarily it negates the act which presupposes the possibility. Therefore "impossible" is opposed both to "possible" and to "necessary."

[69]

Secondly, it follows that the aforementioned modes are syncategorematic words. The reason is that they determine the composition itself by amplifying, as was said. Therefore they are qualities of the predicate insofar as it is the predicate. For there are two kinds of qualities of the subject or of the predicate. A subject and a predicate are taken in one way for that which is the subject and for that which is the predicate; in another way for the subject insofar as it is the subject and for the predicate insofar as it is the predicate. Thus some are qualities of that which is the subject and of that which is the predicate; others are qualities of the subject and predicate as subject and predicate. For example, when one says: "Every white horse necessarily runs swiftly," "white" and "swiftly" in this case are qualities of that which is the subject and of that which is the predicate. But such words are neither syncategorematic nor do they denominate the proposition; for the proposition is not called "white" or "swift." Rather "every" and "necessarily" are qualities, respectively, of the subject as subject and of the predicate as predicate. Therefore, they are syncategorematic words. Such words denominate the proposition from the point of view of the subject, since from them the proposition is called universal, particular, indesignate, or singular. But the qualities of the predicate as predicate denominate it from the point of view of quality, since from them the proposition is called affirmative or negative, modal or categorical: for from an affirmation of the predicate, the proposition is called affirmative, and from a negation of it, it is called negative; and from a mode determining the composition of the proposition it is called modal but from the inherence alone of a predicate in a subject it is called a categorical proposition. Some rules must now be posited regarding the conversion of the propositions which we discussed.

The first rule is: Every proposition concerning the necessary and the possible and every one concerning the necessarily contingent and the possibly contingent, both affirmative and negative, ought to be converted in the same way as those categoricals, namely, a universal negative and a particular affirmative, simply; a universal affirmative proposition not simply but *per accidens;* and a particular negative proposition cannot be converted in its terms. Nevertheless, one must understand that the aforementioned propositions are not converted in their entirety since in modal propositions the mode is always predicated. Rather they are converted from the point of view of what was stated, by making the stated subject predicate and *vice versa;* as for example: "That no man be a stone is necessary," therefore "That no stone be a man is necessary."

Another rule is: All propositions concerning the non-necessary contingent, both affirmatives and negatives, can be converted into the opposite quality. The reason is that just as contingent propositions are able to be, they can also not be; for example, if "It is contingent that every man be white," then "It is contingent that no man be white." But one converts to an opposite quality when another proposition of an opposite quality follows from an affirmative or a negative proposition. However, this conversion is made differently according to the different modes of the contingent. For a proposition concerning the indefinite contingent is converted into another of the same contingency; but that concerning the naturally contingent is converted into one of rare contingency and, conversely, one of rare contingency is converted into the naturally contingent; for example, "It is contingent that some man become gray in old age," therefore "It is contingent that some man not become gray in old age."

Another rule is: Affirmative propositions concerning the non-necessary contingent are converted in the same way with respect to terms as those which are categorical; negatives on the other hand are not. For a universal negative is not converted simply by virtue of the fact that a universal negative follows from a universal affirmative by converting it into an opposite quality; but if this negative were converted simply into a universal negative, on the other hand, a universal affirmative follows from that negative in accordance with an opposed quality; therefore, from the first to the last, a universal affirmative would follow from a universal affirmative, and thus one would argue from the undistributed to the distributed. But a particular negative proposition concerned with such a contingency is converted simply, because it is equivalent to a particular affirmative proposition which is converted simply.

Another rule is: Propositions concerning the impossible ought to be converted in the same way as those concerning the necessary, with which they are equivalent.

With regard to what has been said, this sophism is discussed: "If Sortes is mortal necessarily, he is immortal necessarily." *The proof:* If Sortes is mortal, Sortes is some kind of thing necessarily. And if Sortes is some kind of thing necessarily, Sortes is immortal necessarily. Therefore, from the first to the last: "If Sortes is mortal necessarily, Sortes is immortal necessarily."

To the contrary: In this case an opposite follows from an opposite. Therefore the statement is impossible.

Solution: The antecedent of that conditional is ambiguous, namely, "Sortes is mortal necessarily." For the word "necessarily" can in one way determine the composition and then the sense is: "This proposition: 'Sortes is mortal,' is necessary." In another way it can determine the predicate and in a twofold manner: in one way it can determine the predicate from the point of view of a natural disposition which it implies and then the sense is: "Sortes has a necessary natural disposition toward or aptitude for death"; in the other way it can determine the predicate from the point of view of the act in relation to which it affirms the natural disposition and then the sense is: "Sortes has a natural disposition such that he dies necessarily." In the two first senses, the antecedent of the first conditional is impossible and the consequent follows. Also in these two ways the sophism is true. But an opposite does not follow from an opposite, rather one part of a contradiction follows from an antecedent which includes both simultaneously. In the third sense the antecedent is true but the consequent does not follow. Therefore the sophism is false and the disproof holds. To the proof one answers that it does not follow that "Sortes is immortal necessarily; therefore he is some kind of thing necessarily," because it does not follow that "Sortes is moved of necessity; therefore Sortes is some kind of thing necessarily." In that case there is a fallacy of passing from the relative to the absolute.

In like manner, positing that there are three souls which always remain just and that one unjust soul is created, then this sophism is discussed: "Every soul is just necessarily." *The proof:* This soul is just necessarily; also that one and that one. But there are no more, because that which will be in the future, is not yet. Therefore "Every soul is just necessarily."

To the contrary: "Every soul is just"—this proposition will be false in the future. Therefore, a mode of necessity having been apposed, it is false.

Solution: The initial statement is ambiguous. Indeed, in one way it can be understood with a restriction of the subject term to the present souls, so that the sense is: "Every soul, which now is, is just necessarily," and then it is true. In another way it can be understood without a restriction of the subject and then it is false—as is clear from the disproof—to understand still that "necessarily" determines the composition.

From what has been said, the senses of propositions in which the mentioned modes are posited can be understood. For it was stated how these modes can amplify composition and by this vary the sense of a categorical proposition. However, regarding this some rules must be noted.

The first rule is: Whenever two determinations of the composition are posited in the same statement, the statement is ambiguous due to the fact that one can be a determination of the other or vice versa, for example: "Sortes does not run necessarily." This is ambiguous due to the fact that the negation can determine the necessity or the

[72]

necessity can determine the negation, as is obvious from this: "Sortes does not run contingently."

The second rule is: As often as the word "necessarily" is posited in the consequent of some conditional, the proposition is ambiguous; for example, "If Sortes runs, he is moved necessarily," [is ambiguous] by reason of the fact that it can affirm the necessity of the consequence and then the sense is: "If Sortes runs, it follows necessarily that he is moved," or it can affirm the necessity of the proposition which is the consequent and then the sense is: "If Sortes runs, this proposition is necessary: 'Sortes is moved' "—which is false.

Another rule is: As often as the word "necessarily" is posited in a proposition disjunctive of immediate contraries or of contradictories, the proposition is ambiguous by reason of the fact that it can affirm the necessity of the disjunctives or the necessity of the disjunctive parts; as for example: "Sortes runs; necessarily in the future he will run or he will not run."

Another rule is: As often as this verb "is contingent" is apposed to accidental terms, the statement is ambiguous by reason of the fact that it can affirm the contingency of the predicate but not of the subject or it can affirm the contingency of both, for example: "Everything white contingently runs." If it affirms the contingency of the predicate only, the sense is: "Everything which is white contingently runs." If, however, it affirms the contingency of both the subject and the predicate, the sense is: "Everything which contingently is white contingently runs," and then the mode is implied in relation to the subject. Therefore Aristotle[12] distinguishes in the first book of the *Prior Analytics:* "Every *b* contingently is *a*," for in one way the sense is: "Everything which is *b* contingently is *a*"; in another way the sense is: "Everything which contingently is *b*, contingently is *a*" etc.

Having discussed "necessarily" and "contingently," we must as a consequence discuss the conjunction "or" *(an)*. There are many genera of conjunctions. Some are genera of dubitative conjunction according to Priscian,[13] as, for example, "or" *(an)*, "whether" *(utrum)*, "Is it the case that" *(ne)*. And Donatus[14] includes this genus of conjunction under the disjunctives. But, omitting other interrogatives and dubitatives, our present intent is to treat of the conjunction "or" *(an)*, which, the same as regards substance, nevertheless is different as regards understanding. It exercises three acts, which are to interrogate and to doubt and to disjoin. Accordingly it belongs to different species of conjunc-

---

[12] *Analytica priora* i. 13. 40ª 25 sqq.

[13] *Inst. Gram.*, xvi, 12. 9.

[14] *The Ars Minor of Donatus,* translated by Wayland Johnson Chase, in University of Wisconsin Studies in the Social Sciences and History, no. 11. (Madison: 1926) p. 50. (All subsequent references to Donatus are from this study).

tion. For as it disjoins, it is then contained under the disjunctive species. It is also contained under the same species when we interrogate by it. However, if we doubt by it, it is contained under the dubitative disjunctive species. And among these acts, to disjoin belongs to it primarily and to be interrogative and dubitative posteriorly, for it always disjoins but it does not always doubt or interrogate.

It must be noted, however, that it is possible to doubt in three ways. Sometimes it is possible to doubt concerning the thing signified by a noun *(nomen)*, whether it is signified by the substantive or by the adjective. One asks about such by means of interrogative pronouns, such as "who" *(quis)*, "whoever" *(quaeque)*, "what kind" *(qualis)*, "how great" *(quantus)*, "how many" *(quotus)*, according to the diversity of substance and of those things which modify a substance. Certainly there is doubt at times concerning a specific act. And then one asks about it by means of the interrogative "what" *(quid)* added to the generic act; for example, to "What is he doing?" one replies "He is sitting," "He is sleeping," "He is arguing," or "He is reading." And in the case of these two modes one asks about the dubitative thing by means of nouns. For sometimes we doubt concerning what determines an act, for example, concerning the cause of an act, as when one is reading, "Why is he reading?"; or concerning the time in which an act happens, as "When will he run?"; or concerning a place "Where is he producing?"; "Whence is he coming?"; "Where is he going?", "Whither has he passed?" One asks about these by means of locative adverbs. And thus it is clear that as far as all the words which determine an act are concerned, one asks a question by means of adverbs. Also, we sometimes doubt concerning the inherence of an act in or the composition of an act with a substance and then we ask a question by means of interrogative conjunctions, namely, by these, "or" *(an)*, "is it the case that" *(-ne)*, "whether" *(utrum)*, and so forth. Thus it is clear how interrogative conjunctions differ from the others in this, that they ask a question concerning the composition of an act with a substance. This characteristic belongs to these three: "Or," "is it the case that," "whether." They differ, however, in this, that the conjunction "is it the case that" refers rather to the act, whereas "or" and "whether" refer rather to the substance. Hence "is it the case that" asks a question about a particular composition insofar as it is the form of a part and has the mode of an act, whereas "or" and "whether" ask a question about a particular composition insofar as it is the form of a whole and has the mode of a substance. The proof of this is that that concerning which the question arises cannot receive over and above itself the transit *(transitum)* of another act, but that concerning which "or" and "whether" inquire can. And the cause of this is that an act only passes

[74]

over to a substance or that having the mode of substance. Hence this statement means nothing: "You see is it the case that *(ne)* Sortes is running." However one does say: "You see whether *(an)* *(or if [utrum])* Sortes is running." Another difference is that "Is it the case that *(ne)*" is always understood interrogatively, but "or" *(an)* and "whether" *(utrum)* are sometimes understood disjunctively, for example, "I know well whether (or if) Plato reads or does not read." But "or" *(an)* and "whether" *(utrum)* differ because "whether" *(utrum)* is not repeated by itself but requires another conjunctive with it, for example, "You know whether *(utrum)* Sortes is running or *(vel)* Plato"; on the contrary "or" *(an)* can be repeated by itself without another conjunction, as "You know whether *(an)* Sortes is running or *(an)* Plato."

With regard to this conjunction "or" *(an)*, the following rule is cited: As often as "or" *(an)* is posited once in a proposition, it disjoins the opposites of a contradiction; but whenever it is posited twice, it disjoins immediate contraries. The truth of one part of a disjunctive is required determinately on account of the fact that it is customarily affirmed that it is necessary for the respondent to know one part determinately, because, since he ought to certify to the one asking about the question, he ought to be more certain than the interrogator who knows one part generically and universally. Therefore, it is necessary for the respondent to know one part determinately.

The cause of the rule regarding the first part is that in every interrogation something is denoted in the universal concerning which a question is asked in regard to the particular; for example, when one asks: "Who is arguing?" it is denoted that someone is arguing and the question is to certify that someone in the particular. Just as in the interrogation: "Do you know whether Sortes is running?" something in general is denoted concerning which a question arises, but only if one asks determinately about one part of a contradiction which one wishes to be certified. For with regard to that there is a doubt as to why something in general relative to that is denoted by the interrogation. But there is nothing in general from the point of view of a contradiction unless it is the whole divided into the two parts of a contradiction, because the undivided is denoted as between the parts of the contradiction. But this is not really the case unless by virtue of the conjunction "or" *(an)*. Therefore the conjunction "or" *(an)* divides between the parts of a contradiction. But for this mode it is only posited once and it effects a disjunction between the statements opposed as contradictories. Hence this conjunction is interrogative by virtue of an interrogation joined to the disjunction. Whenever there is a disjunction from one part of a contradiction, the result is that the other part is understood, for whenever one doubts regarding one of the

[75]

opposites, he doubts about the other. But in this way it is not a matter of conjunctions which are disjunctive only and not interrogative, as in the case of: "Nothing is stated or Sortes is running," because one of the extremes is lacking. Yet we correctly say: "You know whether Sortes is running."

The second part of the rule is obvious, namely, "whenever it is posited twice, it disjoins statements," for by the interrogation all that is sought is that by which and only that by which in a given reply the question is determined. But, either of the two assertibles concerning which the question is formed having been declared, the question is determined. The identical question, therefore, indifferently asks about this or that. Therefore the word "whether" *(an)* disjoins the things concerning which the question arises. But these are immediate statements. Therefore the second part is true.

Hence it must be noted that the rule is generally true whenever this conjunction "whether" *(an)* is placed before the term to which it is adjoined. But whenever it is placed after a general term which has been determined by a universal sign, it disjoins contradictories only: but having been placed after a general term which has been determined by a particular sign, or which has been posited without a sign, it disjoins opposed subcontradictories; but in all other cases, it disjoins opposed contradictories. For the sense is: "You know whether every man is running," that is, "You know that every man is running or is not running." However, the sense of the statement: "You know of every man whether he is running," is: "You know that every man is running or that every man is not running." Just as the sense of "You know whether someone is sleeping" is: "You know that some man is sleeping or is not sleeping." But the sense of this: "You know of some man whether he is sleeping," is: "You know that some man is sleeping or that some man is not sleeping." In relation to a singular term, however, it makes no difference whether it is placed before or after. The reason for this is the force of the negation understood in the word "whether" *(an)*, the nature of the disjunction mediating. Hence an argument from the superior to the inferior involving the conjunction "whether" is valid in the same way as in the case with negation.

With regard to what has been said, this sophism is discussed: "You know whether every man is Sortes or differs from him." *The proof:* You know whether Plato is Sortes or differs from him, and so on. Therefore, the sophism is true.

To the contrary: You know whether every man is Sortes or differs from him. Therefore you know that every man is Sortes or that every man differs from Sortes—each of which is false.

Solution: The initial statement is absolutely false and the proof errs by concluding from an insufficient induction. For in the proposition: "You know whether every man is Sortes or differs from him," there is a twofold unity, because in one part of the disjunction there is one distribution and in the other part, another. Hence the sense is: "You know whether every man is Sortes or every man differs from him." But all the individuals of these two distributions are not asserted in the proof itself, because, in addition to those which it asserts, it ought to assert these: "You know whether Sortes is Sortes and whether every man differs from him; and you know whether Plato is Sortes and whether every man differs from him." But this disjunctive is false, because each part of it is false. And it is the same with regard to all the others which remain. And in this way it ought to assert all the parts of the first distribution, the second distribution remaining whole. And also, conversely, it ought to assert all the parts of the second distribution in such a way that the first distribution would remain whole, for example: "You know whether every man is Sortes or Sortes differs and so on." In another way they ought to embrace the parts, namely, by embracing all the individuals of one with all the individuals of the other, for example: "You know whether Plato is Sortes or Sortes differs; whether Plato differs from Sortes and so on." But it embraces none of all of these. And thus it is based on an insufficient induction and so errs in concluding. In like manner also "whether" *(an)*, posited once, disjoins opposed contradictories, as is clear enough, etc.

The conjunction "or" *(vel)* is one which does not signify a comparison according to the prior and the posterior but only a comparison of simultaneously existing things by disjoining any two things with respect to some third, so that the conjunction "is" posits the disjuncts to exist simultaneously and it is indifferently related to each. But it does not posit that with respect to which the disjunction exists, as simultaneously existing in them. Hence, when Sortes or Plato is running, Sortes and Plato are posited simultaneously as mutually existing; nevertheless they are not posited simultaneously as running. One ought to understand the statement of Boethius[15] in this way when he says that the disjunctive conjunction means this because it does not allow those things which it conjoins to exist simultaneously. It is the same in the case of the definition of Priscian[16] when he says disjunctive conjunctions are those which, although they conjoin words, nevertheless disjoin meanings. Indeed, they signify that one thing is, but that the other is not. Thus it is clear that the disjunctive con-

---

[15] *De Syllogismo Hypothetico* (PL 64, 834 CD).   [16] *Inst. Gram.*, xvi, 7, 17-18.

junction signifies that things exist simultaneously but it disjoins them with respect to a third.

Sometimes an assertion is made in a properly disjunctive manner as when one disjoins things which cannot be true simultaneously, for example, "Sortes is running or he is not running"; sometimes under a disjunction as whenever one disjoins things which can be validly true at the same time, for example, "Sortes or Plato is running." Therefore some posit this rule: Whenever this conjunction "or" *(vel)* is posited once in a proposition, then the truth of one part indeterminately is required and suffices for the truth of the proposition, for example: "Sortes is running or he is not running"; but whenever "or" *(vel)* is posited twice, the truth of one determinate part is required in order that the proposition itself be true, for example: "Either Sortes is running or Plato." Hence it is not valid to argue from the proposition in which it is posited once to the proposition in which it is posited twice, for it does not follow that "You know that the stars are equal or unequal; therefore you know that the stars either are equal or are unequal."

Whence it must be noted that these three disjunctive conjunctions *"vel," "-ve,"* and *"aut"* *("or")* differ from the three mentioned above, namely, *"an," "-ne," and "utrum"* *("or")*. First, because the former are only disjunctives and not interrogatives, but these three, namely, *"an," "-ne,"* and *"utrum"* are disjunctives and interrogatives, as was revealed in the preceding section. Secondly, these words *"vel," "ve,"* and *"aut"* cannot be a means by which one act can pass over to another act, as is the case with the other three, for example, there is no statement in the case of: "You know or *(vel)* Sortes runs," "You know or *(aut)* Sortes runs," so that the act of knowing would be understood to pass over to what I am saying, [namely], "Sortes runs." An example of correct speech is: "You know whether *(an)* Sortes is running," that is, "You know that Sortes is running or *(vel)* he is not running," "You know whether *(utrum)* Sortes is running," and you may ask "Is *(-ne)* Sortes running?" But *"vel"* (or) differs from the conjunction *"aut"* (or) because *"vel"* disjoins things which move the speculative intellect or any other capacity, only a positive one and not motivated either by an affection or by an appetite, nay rather only according as it is cognitive. But the disjunction *"aut"* disjoins things moving the practical intellect or an affection of it or things moving the sensible appetite. Likewise the conjunction *"-ve"* differs from the other two, namely, *"vel"* and *"aut,"* because it is an enclitic disjunctive conjunction, (while) *"vel"* and *"aut"* are not enclitics. For the enclitic is found only in three conjunctions, namely, *"-que," "-ve,"* and *"-ne."* And they are called enclitics because they restrict or sharpen the accent of the preceding word as regards the last syllable, for example, *"putasne?"* ("Is it the case that you think?"), *"dicitive"* ("or he says"), "amabitque" ("and he will love"). Therefore they always follow the first word of the clause in which they are posited. And on that account they are mentioned under disjunction by Donatus.[17]

Regarding what has been said, this sophism is discussed: "Whatever is, is or is not." *The proof*: Whatever is, is. That is true. And a truth can be distinguished from any other truth. Therefore the initial statement is true.

To the contrary: Whatever is or is not, is. But Caesar is or is not. Therefore Caesar is.

Solution: The initial proposition is ambiguous due to the fact that it can be divided and thus the sense is: "Whatever is, is; or whatever is not, is"—but taken in this way it is true, because it is true as regards one part and so is a disjunctive; or it can be composite and thus the sense is: "Whatever is or is not, is," so that both that which is and that which is not, is—but in this way it is false and categorical. Hence there is a fallacy of division and composition, because the composite is false.

This sophism is discussed: "Every proposition or its contradictory is true." *The proof:* The proposition "Sortes runs" or its contradictory is true and so forth. Therefore the initial proposition is true.

To the contrary: Every proposition etc. Therefore every proposition is true for the contradictory of any proposition whatever is true. But it is not the case that every proposition is true. Therefore the contradictory of any proposition whatever is true. But this is false. Therefore the initial proposition is false.

Solution: The initial proposition is ambiguous due to the fact that disjunctive conjunction can conjoin terms or propositions. If it conjoins propositions, then it is false, as is proved. And the disjunction involves a disjunction previously made relative to "any proposition whatever"; and the same thing, namely, "any proposition whatever" is implied by the relative "its." Or it can disjoin the terms and in this way it is true, as is proved. Thus the disjunction is such that it distributes only the first part of the disjunction as it relates to things denoted in comparison to another, namely, relative to another part understood as any contradictory whatever. But a proposition has the nature of one part of a contradiction, as Aristotle asserts in the first book of the *De Interpretatione*,[18] and then the relative "its" is related to the other part of the contradiction corresponding to it by referring individual for individual, because the whole falls under the disjunction.

[17] *The Ars Minor of Donatus, op. cit.,* p. 50.   [18] *De Interpret.* 6.   17ª   31-33.

Having spoken of this disjunctive conjunction "or" *(vel)*, we now treat of the copulative conjunction "and" which is called copulative not because it signifies a connection but because it signifies a comparison which exists simultaneously or according to simultaneity. And the connection follows from simultaneity just as exclusion naturally follows from my expression "not with another." Hence when I say: "Sortes and Plato are white," the conjunction "and" affirms their simultaneity and oneness in whiteness. And on that account it unites them in whiteness. It does not however indicate simultaneity in time, because thus this would be false: "Adam and Noah were two men," because they did not exist at the same time; but nevertheless one correctly asserts: "He ran yesterday and he is running today and he will run tomorrow," yet these acts of running do not exist at the same time. But primarily and essentially it affirms the simultaneity of many subjects in one accident insofar as it enjoys being or of many accidents in one subject, for example, "Sortes and Plato are white" and "Sortes is seated and he also is arguing."

Hence it must be noted that "a unit" is spoken of in many ways, for one kind of thing is a unit consisting of matter and form, as man is a composite of body and soul; in another way there is a unit by continuity, for example, a line, a surface, time and any continuum; in a third way there is a unit by grafting, for example, in the case of a tree a unit follows from the grafting of a branch of one tree and the trunk of another tree; in a fourth way by continuity, as it exists where there are two bodies between which there is no intermediate, for example, a finger is contiguous to a finger because there is nothing in between; in a fifth way by a collection, for example, from flesh and bone a third unit comes into existence which is neither wholly flesh nor wholly bone, as are the nerves and the cartilages; in a sixth way by addition, for example, a multitude of stones. And in this last way the conjunction "and" produces unity but not in the other aforementioned ways. Thus the copulated term is one by addition. But this union though absolute, the conjunction "and" diversifies, because at times it is opposed to unity, for example, "Man is a body and a soul," and the copulate whole produces a unit by the unity of the individual. Therefore it can be subject to a verb which is singular in number, for example, "A rational soul and flesh constitute one man." Sometimes it is held copulatively in the proper sense and then only does it conjoin diverse objects which enjoy difference among themselves but agreement with respect to something else. Because the conjunction "and" refers equally to each of the extremes, for this reason, whenever it is placed in front of one of the extremes, it is necessary that it be repeated and placed before the other extreme in order that it may be related equally to each, and that it not be related more to that before which it is placed. The copulate whole then produces a unit by addition and posits a multitude absolutely. Then alone is it subject to a verb of plural number, for example, "Sortes and Plato are running."

Further, note that although this conjunction "and" ought to connect different things, it nevertheless does not connect anything whatever, because it does not join an adjective to a substantive, nor vice versa, for example, "A white man is running," because of the fact that, of itself, it affirms a certain conjoining or association of something or other with some kind of a thing. Hence it is equally related to each. And so the cause of every copulative conjunction, except an enclitic, is its equal reference to each of the extremes. Therefore, primarily and essentially the conjunction "and" conjoins two substances to one act or two acts to one substance, as, for example, "Sortes and Plato are white" or "The man is reading and also arguing." Hence, although this conjunction "and" more properly conjoins different subjects and different things which are signified as similarly conditioned, for example, "A man and a horse are running," it can, nevertheless, conjoin different subjects with a unified signification, for example, "A man and a man are running," because in the case of general terms the plural repeats its singular. But one correctly says: "Men are," therefore one correctly says: "A man and a man are." Moreover such are the subjects as are permitted by their predicates. But when one affirms: "A man and a man are running," the predicate requires that the term "man" be held for different men. But if it is held for different men, one correctly says: "A man and a man are running."

Regarding the above, this sophism is discussed: "Every non-animal which with Sortes constitute two, is not Sortes." *The proof:* This non-animal which with *(et)* Sortes constitute two, is not Sortes. Pointing to wood: "That non-animal which with *(et)* Sortes constitute two, is not Sortes"; pointing to a stone and so on. Therefore, "Every non-animal which with *(et)* Sortes constitute two, is not Sortes."

To the contrary: Every non-animal etc. Therefore everything other than an animal which with Sortes constitute two, is not Sortes—this is a topical argument from the convertible because "non-animal" and "other than an animal" are equipollent. But Sortes is an "other than an animal" which with Sortes constitute two. Therefore Sortes is not Sortes—in the fourth mood of the first figure.

Solution: The initial proposition is absolutely true and the disproof is not valid. Nor is it a syllogism which it offers, but rather a paralogism, because the major and the minor premises are ambiguous. For the proposition which was the major premise, namely, "Everything

other than an animal which with Sortes constitute two, is not Sortes"
is ambiguous due to the fact that the relative "which" *(quod)* can
refer to the term "other" or to the term "animal." If, however, it refers
to the term "other," then the major premise is true and the sense is:
"Everything other than an animal which, namely, other than an animal, with Sortes constitute two, is not Sortes." And this is true; there
is nothing other than an animal except stone, wood, and so forth
with respect to all the other inanimate objects, none of which is Sortes.
If, however, the "which" refers to the term "animal," then the major
premise is false and the sense is: "Everything other than an animal
which, namely, an animal, with Sortes constitutes two, is not Sortes."
This, however, is false because Sortes does not raise the number when
taken with himself, rather all other men raise the number when taken
with Sortes, also the other animals; and so Sortes is other than any
animal whatever raising the number when taken with Sortes. But
then he is understood in this distribution: "Everything other than an
animal which, namely, an animal etc." Hence in this way the major
premise affirms that Sortes is not Sortes. But conversely, one must say
of the minor premise that if the relative "which" refers to the term
"animal," it is false. And this, the following situation having been
posited, that there are only two animals, namely, Sortes and a goat,
and "other" is taken to stand for Sortes and the goat, then the minor
is false, because it is affirmed that Sortes is other than these two,
namely, than Sortes and Plato or an animal which is a man. In order
that the falsity of the major may be more obvious in the second sense,
one could posit that Sortes is and no other animal is than Plato and
one horse. Then there is no animal which could raise the number
when taken with Sortes except Plato and that horse. But Sortes is
other than these two and then it is false that: "Every other animal
than these two animals which, namely, animals, raise the number when
taken with Sortes, is not Sortes."

This sophism is discussed: "Every assertible differs from another
and its opposite is compatible with it." *The proof:* The assertible
"Sortes is" differs from another and its opposite is compatible with it
because it differs from the assertible "the horse runs." Also its opposite, namely "Sortes is not," is compatible with it because it can
stand with it. For these two assertibles can be true at the same time,
namely, "Sortes is not" and "the horse runs." That assertible, "the
horse runs," differs from another and its opposite is compatible with
it and so forth. Therefore the initial proposition is true.

To the contrary: This is one copulative of which each part is false;
therefore it is itself false.

Solution: The initial proposition is false and the proof errs by a

[82]

fallacy of figure of speech in passing from many determinate things to one determinate thing by virtue of the term "another." And also there is in this case a fallacy of accident because of a rule which holds in relation to distributions, that although this distribution "every assertible" as such follows convertibly with regard to its singular parts, yet it is all the parts as they are contained under this predicate "differs from another." Thus it does not follow with regard to them, rather there is in this case a fallacy of accident.

We now discuss the word "except" *(nisi)*. Speakers generally posit that the word "except" *(nisi)* properly and naturally is understood consecutively and not exceptively. Therefore, regarding the word "except" itself, one first asks whether the word "except" can be understood exceptively or not; second, one asks whether the word "except" and this phrase "if . . . not" *(si . . . non)* are equivalent to each other, since the word "except" *(nisi)* is compounded of "if" *(si)* and "not" *(non)*; third, one asks how many genera are there of the instantive and how do they differ in genus; fourth, one asks why is an instantive word which is an exceptive word made from the adverb "not" *(non)* by composition rather than an instantive word of another genus; fifth, one asks why should this word "except" insofar as it is universally consecutive, always be adjoined to a verb in the subjunctive mood.

Regarding the first question it is objected that sometimes it is understood exceptively because an instance sometimes happens in relation to a whole as against a part, sometimes an instance happens in the case of a part; for example, when one says: "Every man is running except that Sortes is not running or some man is not running." For in this case an instance happens in the case of a part over against a whole. But positing that Sortes is running and nothing else, this is true: "No man is running except Sortes." But in this case there is an instance by pulling out or separating a part from a whole through the exceptive word "except." Therefore the word "except" is understood exceptively in the aforementioned proposition.

Moreover, in the same relation, when one says: "No man is running except that ass," this is improper. But if the word "except" is understood exceptively, then it would be proper. But it will be false. Therefore the word "except" is not understood consecutively. But it is understood consecutively or exceptively. Therefore it is understood exceptively.

Also, in the same relation, there is a twofold kind of consequence because one is a consequence absolutely, for example: "If a man runs, an animal runs"; another is a consequence as of now *(ut nunc)*, as "If you will come to me, I will give you the church." But from none of these is the antecedent or the consequent inferred, for the conse-

[83]

quence: "Therefore a man runs," which is the antecedent, does not follow from the original statement; nor does it follow that: "Therefore an animal runs," which is the consequent. From the other consequence, which is a consequence *ut nunc*, it does not follow that "Therefore you will come with me," which is the antecedent; nor does it follow that "Therefore I will give you the church," which is the consequent. Therefore, from none of these does the antecedent or the consequent follow. But when one says "no man except Sortes," it validly follows from this that "Therefore the word 'except' is not understood consecutively in this case but rather is understood exceptively." This we concede, saying that "except" is sometimes understood exceptively, as in the aforementioned propositions and exactly similar ones, but it is not always understood consecutively.

To the contrary: This word "except" *(nisi)* is compounded from "if" *(si)* and "not" *(non)*. But neither "if" nor "not" are exceptive words, nor have they the nature of exception. Therefore the word "except" does not have the nature of exception, since the composite may not have any nature except from its components. Hence "except" is never understood exceptively. But it is understood exceptively or consecutively. Therefore it is understood consecutively.

Further, every exceptive word affirms a relation of the parts to a whole. But no conjunction affirms a relation of a part to a whole. Therefore no conjunction is exceptive—in the second mood of the second figure. Therefore the word "except" is not exceptive. But it is exceptive or consecutive. Therefore it is consecutive.

It must be said, as it was previously, that the word "except" is sometimes understood exceptively and sometimes consecutively. But to that which is objected in the contrary argument, one must answer that, just as it is objected, the word "except" *(nisi)* is compounded of "not" *(non)* and "if" *(si)*. But the adverb "not" always requires an exception *(instantiam)* to that to which it is adjoined, since it always contradicts it. Therefore it is an instantive word. It requires an exception, sometimes in relation to a whole, sometimes in a relation to a part, just as we said before. But in the course of composition it is referred to an exception, which exists in relation to a part, by extracting the part from a whole. And this suffices for an exceptive word, for example, "No man is running except Sortes." Therefore the word "except" is sometimes understood exceptively and sometimes consecutively. Thus it is clear that although the adverb "not" is not an exceptive word, nevertheless it has an instantive nature, which instantive nature is reduced in the course of composition to an instance of exceptive words in the case of the word "except" *(nisi)*.

Moreover, to the second objection set forth in the contrary argu-

[84]

ment, one must answer that there was not a syllogism in the second mood of the second figure but rather a paralogism. For the minor of the aforementioned paralogism is ambiguous, namely, this: "No conjunction affirms a relation of a part to a whole," due to the fact that there are some conjunctions which have in themselves an ambiguous nature, as is the case with those conjunctions which are composed of conjunctions and other parts of speech, for example, the conjunction "on account of which" *(quapropter)* which is composed of the word "which" *(qua)* and the preposition "on account of" *(propter)*. Thus the comprehension of it is constituted of the comprehensions of those words. This conjunction "except," moreover, is a composite, as was said, of "not" and "if." Hence it has in itself the nature of the instantive which is concerned with a part and in virtue of this it affirms a relation of the part to a whole or a comparison. And thus it has in itself a twofold nature, namely, an instantive nature by reason of the adverb from which it is composed, whence it is called an instantive conjunction, but in another way it has a consecutive nature by reason of the conjunction, whence it is called a consecutive conjunction. Also it has an adversative nature from the point of view of consecution, whence it is called an adversative conjunction.

Regarding the second question, as is clear from what has been said, it must be noted that the word "except" *(nisi)* is sometimes understood exceptively, sometimes consecutively. Understood consecutively, the word "except" *(nisi)* and the phrase "if not" *(si non)*, are equivalent, for example, "He does not run, *except* he be moved," that is, "He does not run, *if* he is *not* moved." However, when the word "except" is understood exceptively, it then signifies something other than the phrase "if not." And they do not signify the same thing, since then it would signify the relation of a part to a whole, as for example, "not with this." For just as the exclusive word signifies "this, not simultaneous with another," so, conversely, the exceptive word signifies "the whole, not with this."

Regarding the third question, note that there are three genera of the instantive, for some are exclusive, and so they set apart an instance by excluding; others are exceptive and they set apart an instance by excepting; others are contradictory or contradicting, and through these the instantive or contradictories are made by contradicting. Note that they also differ generically as follows, because exclusives always set apart an instance in relation to a whole by excluding it, as, for example, "Only Sortes is running," whereas exceptives always set apart an instance in the case of a part by always extracting the part from a whole, as "No man except Sortes is running"; contradictories or the contradicting set apart an instance indifferently, sometimes in relation

[85]

to a whole, sometimes in the case of a part, by removing something from a whole or from a part, as "Some man is running," "No man is running," "Every man is running," "Some man is not running."

Regarding the fourth question, since the word "not" is understood in any instantive word whatever, as in exclusive and exceptive words and in contradicting words, since it is a principle of all of them, then, just as an exceptive word arises from it by composition, so also ought an instantive word of another genus arise from it, as, for example, an exclusive. It must be said that the word "not" is not to be understood in the same way in the case of any instantive whatever. Hence it is not a principle of all instantive words in one way. For one word is the principle of another in a twofold manner: in one way by addition but in another way by composition. Hence I say that in the case of exclusive words, negation is understood by their addition, because "only" and "alone" by reason of their addition signify "not with another." And those exceptive words, "with the exception of," "except," are understood similarly by reason of the addition of negation. But the contradicting words "none," "nothing," "neither," and even the exceptive word "except," exist by composition, although the others exist by addition.

Similarly, one asks why an exceptive word arises by composition from the adverb "not" and from the conjunction "if" rather than an exclusive word since the adverb "not" is instantive and an instance is found both in the case of exceptive and exclusive words, although indifferently. And it must be said that the adverb "not" is a negative because it denies, but the adversative is understood when it is taken in successive relation to the word "if." Hence in the word "except" (*nisi*), negation and the adversative is understood. A word is exceptive by virtue of the fact that it is opposed to what precedes as regards any part of it.

Again, since the word "except" (*nisi*) is always a composite of "not" (*non*) and "if" (*si*), and since it is sometimes exceptive [and] some-times consecutive, it is therefore necessary that the composition of the word "except" be made in several ways from its components. This we concede, saying that whenever the word "except" is consecutive, it destroys the negation. Then the consecution of this word "except" is complete. But then, according to Priscian,[19] this word is included under the continuative conjunction (*coniunctione continuativa*), where-as, according to Donatus,[20] it is included under the causal conjunction: for example, "He does not run, except he be moved," that is, "If he is not moved, he does not run." But whenever it is exceptive, the

[19] *Inst. Gram.*, xvi, 3. [20] *The Ars Minor of Donatus*, *op. cit.*, p. 52.

negation destroys the consecution. And then the negation changes the composition into another species, because it is in the exceptive word. So in accordance with the different ways of composition, the word "except" belongs to one and to another species.

If it be asked whether an instance is found equally in the three aforementioned genera of instantive words, it must be said that it is not the case because an instance is primarily characteristic of contradicting instantive words—and this is composition in the highest degree, when there is a composition present; but an instance is found secondarily in exceptive words; and yet it is in these more than in exclusives. And although any exception does not immediately contradict its whole, nevertheless a contradiction does follow; for example, from "Every man except Sortes is running," it follows that "Sortes is not running," and it further follows that "Some man is not running"—and it is a topical argument from a subjective part. But in the case of exceptive words, that which is excluded does not contradict that from which the exclusion is made, for example, "Sortes alone is running," that is, "No one other than Sortes is running." For these two propositions: "Sortes is running," "No one other than Sortes is running," do not contradict, neither immediately nor consequently. Therefore, an instance is less characteristic of exclusive words but more of exceptive words and most of all of contradicting words.

Concerning the fifth question, one objects that the conjunction is naturally fit to connect the other parts of speech, therefore both nouns and verbs; and as regards the other parts of speech, both any numbers whatever and any person whatever and any tenses whatever and any mood whatever; also as regards the other parts of speech under these and other accidental characteristics. Therefore the word "except" (nisi), inasmuch as it is a consecutive conjunction, is erroneously limited to the subjective mood alone.

Solution: One must say that the negation which exists in the word "except" (nisi) is not an absolute but a relative negation, inasmuch as the word "except" is a consecutive word. The reason for this is that negation and consecution are certainly united in the one intellection of the word "except." Since intellection exists in consecution, the negation exists in consecution, for it is united in the one intellection with the consecution itself, as we said. Therefore the negation is not absolute in this case but relative. Hence, since negation ought to determine the verb, therefore absolute negation will determine the verb to be absolute and relative negation in speech will determine the verb to be relative. And since among all the moods of verbs the subjunctive mood alone affirms its subject (rem) in relation to or in comparison with another, it follows that the word "except," inasmuch as it is consecutive, ought to be adjoined to a verb in the subjunctive mood.

In accordance with the aforementioned, this sophism is discussed: "Nothing is true except in this instance" *(instanti). The proof:* Whatever is true in this instance, is true. Therefore nothing is true except in this instance.

To the contrary: Nothing is true except in this instance. Therefore your being an ass is not true except in this instance. Therefore your being an ass in this instance, is true. Therefore you are an ass.

Or it can be proved as follows: Nothing can be true. And there is no instance except for what is true in this instance. Therefore, an exception having been made for that, it will be true. Therefore this is true: "Nothing is true except in this instance."

Solution: The initial statement is ambiguous due to the fact that the word "except" *(nisi)* can be understood exceptively or consecutively. And in each way it is true, "instance" having been understood generally, whether in relation to the instance itself, or in relation to the now itself, or in relation to the present time. But the initial statement itself must be distinguished, and one must reply in different ways to the arguments of the disproof. Therefore, we must first consider each sense. Second, we must consider what we shall reply to the disproof. Hence, the sense of the initial statement, in accordance with its being exceptive, is as follows: "Nothing is true except in this instance," that is, "Nothing is true with the exception of the true in this instance." This is true, truth being understood universally for the true which exists in this instance and for the true which exists in time; just as the instance is understood generally in relation to the present and in relation to time. If, moreover, the initial statement is understood consecutively, the sense is: "Nothing is true except in this instance," that is, "Nothing is true, if it is not true in this instance." In this way again the initial proposition is true. Therefore, the distinction having been made, one must assert in reply to the disproof that, insofar as the initial statement is exceptive, the first argument of the disproof does not hold, namely: "Nothing is true except in this instance. Therefore your being an ass is not true except in this instance," because there is in this case a sophism involving a fallacy of accident, just as in the following case: "No man with the exception of Sortes is running. Therefore Plato with the exception of Sortes is running." For in this way the initial proposition is categorical and the distribution "nothing" comprehends under itself both the true and the false, both the complex and the incomplex. Hence "true in this instance" is excepted from the distribution understood in this fashion. Whence "true in this instance" is part of that distribution, but it is not part of that which I am affirming, "your being an ass," just as Sortes is a part of the distribution "no man" but he will not be a part of Plato. If, however, one understands the initial statement consecutively, the first argument of the disproof holds validly, namely, "Nothing is true except in this instance. Therefore your being an ass is not true except in this instance," because the sense is: "Nothing is true, if it is not true in this instance." But the argument which follows does not hold, namely: "Your being an ass is not true except in this instance," because the sense is: "You are an ass. Therefore 'your being an ass is true in this instance,' is not true, if it is not true in this instance. Therefore your being an ass is true in this instance." Either there is no demonstration (*apparentia*) in this case, or the argument is wholly contradictory, or there is a fallacy of the qualified and absolute statement in virtue of the fact that from no conditional does one validly infer the antecedent and the consequent. For example, "If a man runs, an animal runs"; from this it does not therefore follow: "A man runs" or "An animal runs." Similarly, the following is a *non-sequitur*: "Your being an ass is not true except in this instance. Therefore your being an ass is true in this instance," because here one posits the antecedent and thus there is in this case a fallacy of the qualified and absolute statement. Furthermore, one can still say that there is no demonstration in this case, because from a negated antecedent and a negated consequent one is inferring an affirmative consequent, for example: "If an animal does not exist, a man does not exist; therefore an animal is a man." For in this affirmation, there is no demonstration, as we said, or there is in this case a fallacy of the qualified and absolute statement.

The problem of the following sophism is discussed: "No man reads a Parisian unless he be an ass." *The proof:* This is false: "Some man reads a Parisian unless he be an ass." Therefore, its contradictory is true, namely, this: "No man reads a Parisian unless he be an ass." But "not some" and "no" are equipollent. Therefore the initial proposition is true.

To the contrary: No man reads a Parisian unless he be an ass. Therefore, by the destruction of the consequent, "If any man reads a Parisian, he is an ass." But this is false. And therefore the initial proposition is false.

Solution: The initial proposition is absolutely false. This is ambiguous: "Some man reads a Parisian, unless he be an ass," due to the fact that the negation can determine the verb of the consequent in itself and absolutely, that is, "reads." And then it is false. In this way they are equivalent to the initial proposition and the sense is: "No man reads" and "From 'no man is an ass' it follows that 'no man reads a Parisian.'" And in this way "not some" and "no" are equivalent. According to this, "It is not the case that some man reads a Parisian unless he be an ass" does not contradict this: "Some man reads a Parisian etc." For each is false. Or one negation can determine the verb of the consequent, that is, "reads," not in itself and absolutely but in relation to the antecedent. Then it is true and the sense is: "It is not the case that some man reads a Parisian etc.," that is, "It does not follow from 'no man is an ass' that 'no man reads a Parisian.'" However in this way the whole consequent is denied, and in the first way only a part. But it does contradict this: "Some man reads a Parisian etc." And in this way it is not equivalent to the first.

The problem of the following sophism is discussed: "No man dies, unless one man alone dies." *The proof:* This is false: "Some man dies, unless one man alone dies." Therefore its contradictory is true: namely, this: "It is not the case that some man dies etc." But "not some" and "no" are equivalent. Therefore the initial proposition is true.

To the contrary: The antecedent is possible but the consequent is impossible. Therefore the conditional is false. That the antecedent is possible is obvious, because it has two causes of its truth or many; for that one man alone does not die is true; but that two die or that many more than two die or even if all die, still the consequent is always false, namely, "No man dies."

The solution is the same as it was in the preceding sophism.

The mode of reduplication is diversified according to the diversity of causes and terms. And therefore it is said universally that this reduplicative "due to the fact that" has different intensions according to the diversity of causes. And on account of this, regarding this reduplicative, we first ask concerning its division according to the diverse genera of causes; second, whether the reduplicative ought to be posited with reference to the subject or the predicate in a proposition; third, we ask in relation to what is it posited in a syllogism, whether in relation to the major, the minor, or the middle term.

Regarding the first, it must be known, as it is generally the custom to say, that this expression "due to the fact that" sometimes affirms an efficient cause: for example: "Sortes and Plato, due to the fact that they are white, are similar," because whiteness in different subjects is the efficient cause of their similarity; again, "Due to the fact that the sun shines over our hemisphere, it is day"; also, "Due to the fact that the earth is an object between the sun and the moon, there is an eclipse." Sometimes, however, it affirms a material cause, for example: "The body of animate things, due to the fact that it is an organic body, is perfectible by the soul." Sometimes, moreover, it affirms a formal cause: for example: "The soul, due to the fact that it is the soul, is the perfection of an organic body having life in potency"; also, "Whiteness is the form of a white object." Again, it sometimes affirms a final cause, for example: "Health, due to the fact that it is health, is the end of medicine and of everything which is related to it"; also, "Virtue, due to the fact that it is virtue, posits the necessity for preceding operations."

Regarding the aforementioned, the problem of the following sophism is discussed: "Some things, due to the fact that they agree, differ." *The proof:* Some things, due to the fact that they agree, are. Due to the fact that they are, they are many. And due to the fact that they are many, they differ. Therefore, according to the original proposition, "Some things, due to the fact that they agree, differ."

To the contrary: To differ and to agree are opposites. Therefore one is not the cause of the other. Therefore the initial proposition is false, because the reduplication "due to the fact that" *(in eo)* asserts that agreement is the cause of difference.

Solution: The initial proposition is absolutely false. Regarding the proof it must be said that it must be explained away by the destruction of this: "Due to the fact that they are, they are many," because it is false. This is obvious, because just as all particular men, due to the fact that they are men, participate in one nature and are reduced to the unity of a species—whence Porphyry[21] says that "by participation in the species many men are one man"—similarly, some or many, due to the fact that they are, participate in the nature of being and are reduced to the truth of being. But due to the fact that they are, it does not follow that they are many; rather it follows that they are one, due to the fact that they are.

If one should object [that] "It is impossible to agree unless the same things also differ, because agreement consists in this, that many things differing among themselves participate in one nature common to them; therefore it is necessary that if they agree, that they should differ," then it must be said that, just as he objects, this is true: "If some things agree, they differ." Nevertheless the initial statement is not true, for agreement does not assert the cause of the difference, rather the determination "due to the fact that" asserts the cause, that agreement is the cause of the difference, as was said. Hence, just as this is true: "If Sortes is a man, Sortes is risible," but yet this is false: "Sortes, due to the fact that he is Sortes, is risible," nay rather "due to the fact that he is a man," so in like manner this is true: "Some things, if they agree, differ," but yet this is false: "Some things, due to the fact that they agree, differ."

---

[21] Cf. Boethius, *In Porphy. Comm.* iii. (PL 64, 111).

The problem of the following sophism is discussed: "Equivocal terms, due to the fact that they are equivocal, are univocal." *The proof:* Equivocal terms, due to the fact that they are equivocal, participate in the name "equivocal" and in its nature. But whatever participates in the name and nature of anything is named univocal in that respect. Therefore, equivocal terms, due to the fact that they are equivocal, are univocal because they are named univocal in being named equivocal. But whatever things are named univocal in relation to something, are univocal. Therefore "Equivocal terms, due to the fact that they are equivocal, are univocal."

To the contrary: Univocal and equivocal are opposites. Of opposites no one is the cause of the other. Therefore this is false: "Equivocal terms, due to the fact that they are equivocal, are univocal," because the determination "due to the fact" *(in eo)* asserts that the subject is the cause of the predicate, which is false.

Solution: The initial proposition is absolutely false. And I concede that "equivocal terms, due to the fact that they are equivocal, are named univocal in being named equivocal." However, it does not follow from this that they are univocal nor that they are named univocal in relation to something. For to be named univocal in relation to equivocity is not to be named univocal absolutely but relatively. Therefore, there is a fallacy of the qualified to the absolute. It is obvious that to be named univocal in being named equivocal is not to be named univocal absolutely but relatively. For whatever things are named univocal, participate in one name and one nature and this is to be named univocal absolutely; but whatever things are named univocal in being named equivocal, participate in one name and different natures; but therefore to be named univocal in being named equivocal is not to be named univocal absolutely but rather to be named equivocal.

Regarding the second question, note that the reduplication as such in a proposition and, more properly speaking, in an assertion ought to be posited relative to the subject, since the subject is the cause of the predicate or it has in it the cause of the predicate, for example, "Sortes, due to the fact that he is a man, is risible"; and "A triangle, due to the fact that it is a triangle, has three angles equal to two right angles"; also "An animal, due to the fact that it has a lung, breathes"; again, "An animal, due to the fact that it has a heart, has blood."

Regarding the third question, note that the reduplication in a syllogism ought to be posited relative to the major extreme, and never relative to the middle nor to the minor term, for example, "Every man is risible due to the fact that he is a man. But Sortes is a man. Therefore, Sortes is risible due to the fact that he is a man." The following is an example of Aristotle's:[22] "For any good whatever there is a science due to the fact that it is a good. But all justice is good. Therefore for any justice whatever there is a science due to the fact that it is a good"—in the first mood of the first figure. And the reduplication is only posited relative to the major extreme and not to the middle term. And it subjoins the cause, asserting that "For the good, due to the fact that it is the good, is to be predicated of justice." It is false and not intelligible. For on account of the fact that the same thing is posited to be the cause of itself, it is false; and because the intellect cannot apprehend the same in essence to be different in essence and prior and posterior in nature to itself, therefore it is not intelligible. Absurdities follow from the proposition: "Justice is good due to the fact that it is good," inasmuch as the predicate is reduplicated relative to itself. For terms following logically are predicated from the point of view of the essence and they function as subject from the point of view of substance, for example, "Man is man." For "man" in the predicate affirms an essence, as Aristotle[23] says, and in the subject it affirms a substance. The same essence, however, cannot be the cause of itself, because then it would be in itself the same and different and prior and posterior in nature, for it would be the cause and the effect. It is affirmed, moreover, that terms affirming an essence, as "man," "animal," and the like, are predicated from the point of view of the essence and function as subjects, from the point of view of the substance, as is obvious in the predicamental order. For example, it is clear in the third line, for according as "man" is ordered in a direct predicamental line above Sortes, Plato, and other individuals, it then names the essence and it is predicated from the point of view of that; but according as "man" is applied to the individuals in which it is realized, then it names substance, just as this individual understood indeterminately is "some man." And therefore whenever "man" functions as subject from the point of view of some inferior, it is then said to function as subject from the point of view of substance.

The number of species of conjunctions, according to Donatus,[24] is five. Indeed there are many species of conjunctions, among which are enumerated the species of causal conjunctions, both by Priscian[25] and by Donatus,[26] and the species of rational conjunctions, which Priscian[27] calls collective or rational. According to Donatus,[28] the con-

22 *Nichomachaean Ethics* i. 1. 1094ª 1 sqq.

23 *Categoriae* 5. 2ª 11 sqq.

24 *The Ars Minor of Donatus, op. cit.* p. 50.

25 *Inst. Gram.,* xvi, 4.

26 *The Ars Minor of Donatus, op. cit.,* p. 50.

27 *Inst. Gram.,* xvi, 11. 15.

28 *The Ars Minor of Donatus, op. cit.,* p. 52.

junction "without" *(quin)* is contained under the causals, but according to Priscian[29] it is contained under the collective or under the rational. Having dismissed this difference for the present because it pertains to grammar, we intend to inquire here, in the first place, whether the conjunction "without" signifies consequence. In the second place, having held that it signifies consequence, whether it signifies any special consequence or a consequence common to all consequences. In the third place, whether this conjunction "without" *(quin)* is composed of the words "that" *(qui)* and "not" *(non)*. In the fourth place, whether it is equivalent to them or is convertible with them. In the fifth place, we ask why the conjunction "without" is always conjoined to a conjunctive verb.

Regarding the first question it is objected that, as Priscian[30] would have it, every conjunction signifies an order or a capacity. Conjunctions signify a capacity which signify that some things exist simultaneously, for example, "Aeneas was pious and brave." They signify an order when they demonstrate the consequence of some things, for example, "If a man walks, he is moved." But this conjunction "without" does not signify that things exist at the same time. Therefore it signifies the consequence of some things. Therefore, it signifies a consequence.

Again, on the same point, this is true: "There is no man without there being an animal." By the conjunction "without" one signifies that it is not possible that there be a man in such wise *that* he be *not* an animal. Therefore it signifies that a man cannot exist without an animal exist. But if a man cannot exist without an animal exist, then "animal" of necessity follows from "man." But this conjunction "without" cannot signify this unless it is a consecutive word. But then it signifies a consequence. Therefore, the conjunction signifies a consequence.

Again, on the same point, Priscian[31] says that conjunctive conjunctions or rational conjunctions are those which connect in inference, just as was said above, and he exemplifies with these, "therefore" *(ergo)*, "so that" *(quod)*, "without" *(quin)*, and with many others. Therefore, the word "without" is an illative word. But a consequent is understood in every inference.

But it is objected to the contrary that the following propositions are generally accepted: "He does not hear the lectures without he sleeps," "He does not eat without he drinks," and others of like kind. But in these, one does not follow of necessity from the other. Therefore the conjunction "without" does not signify an inference nor a consequence.

The answer is that the conjunction "without" does not assert the

---

[29] *Inst. Gram.*, xvi, 11. 15-16.   [31] *Inst. Gram.*, xvi, 11. 15-17.
[30] *Inst. Gram.*, xvi, 1. 1-6.

consecution of an inference. Hence it is a consecutive or an illative word; and we concede all the arguments regarding this. But regarding that which is objected to the contrary, that it is posited generally that the following is true: "He does not hear the lectures without he sleeps," and others of like kind, one might say that consequence is twofold. Hence one is a consequence absolutely, for example: "If a man is, an animal is"; the other is a consequence relative to the present, for example, "If you come to me, I will go with you." And in this second way, it is not necessary that one follows of necessity from the other.

Again, it seems that it does not signify consecution, since, according to Priscian,[32] it is collective or rational. Therefore it signifies an inference but not consecution. And it must be said that everything inferred, insofar as it is inferred, follows, and everything implying, insofar as it is the implying, is antecedent. Hence in every inference, consecution and antecedence are understood. And therefore the word "without" signifies consecution through an inference or in an inference. And thus it signifies one through another or in another. And this is not to signify many things but to signify one thing.

Again, since the word "without" is illative and in every inference antecedence is understood prior to the consecution, because the implying causes the inferred from itself, but not conversely, therefore the word "without" will signify antecedence prior to consecution. It must be said that "without" signifies consecution prior to antecedence. But it does not signify antecedence except from consecution, because consecution cannot exist without antecedence. Moreover, to the objection that in an inference antecedence is prior and consecution is posterior, it must be said that it is true that, since illative words refer more or have a relation to consecution rather than to antecedence due to the fact that an inference looks to a conclusion as an object or terminus "to which" *(ad quem)* and looks to premises as that from which it is or as a terminus "from which" *(a quo),* and because the movement of the mind has its nature and species more from the terminus "to which" *(ad quem)* than from the terminus "from which" *(a quo),* therefore the inference is compared more naturally to that which is inferred or to the conclusion rather than to that which implies or to the premises; hence the conclusion is as the complete or perfect comprehension of the inference; and because of this the word "without," since it is illative, is related more to consecution than to antecedence. Note that the premises, as far as their cognition is concerned, are the efficient cause of the very cognition of the conclusion; but the premises themselves, as far as their substance is concerned, are in one

[32] *Inst. Gram.,* xvi, 11. 15-16.

way the material cause of the conclusion and in another way, as far as their substance is concerned, are the efficient cause of the substance of the conclusion because these same premises, as far as their extremes are concerned, are the matter of the substance of the conclusion. For the major extreme is descended from the premises and so also is the minor extreme so that the conclusion is made from these as from its matter. But the premises, as far as the middle term arranged between each extreme in accordance with its substance is concerned, are the efficient cause of the substance of the conclusion because of the fact that the middle term constitutes the whole efficacy of the premises on the basis of which efficacy the substance of the conclusion is educed or non-being is educed into being. Thus it is clear that in one way the premises are the matter of the conclusion and in two ways are the efficient cause of the conclusion. Note also that in the case of syllogisms composed of contradictories, for example, "Every man is a stone. Every she-goat is a man. Therefore every she-goat is a stone," and universally in the case of any syllogism whatever which consists of false propositions, the premises are not the efficient cause as regards cognition; rather, they are a cause as regards substance, and they also are the material cause, as was said.

Regarding the second question, it is objected that the word "without" *(quin)* asserts only a comparison of one thing to another thing. But in comparison of one to another there is consecution. Similarly, but not composite. Therefore the word "without" only asserts simple but not composite consecution. We concede this, saying that with regard to consecutions, one type is simple, for example, "If a man is, an animal is," as was said in relation to the fallacy of the consequent; another type is composite or manifold, as is the type which exists in accordance with the various kinds of oppositions, just as that which exists in the case of the thing itself or its contrary. Hence we say that the word "without" does not assert a consequence common to the simple and the composite, rather it only signifies that which is simple. But as regards the simple, one is a consequence or a consecution in the absolute sense, as was mentioned previously, but the other is a consequence or a consecution as things are now, i.e., relatively. Hence this word "without" does not signify a consequence universally in relation to all other consequences, rather it only signifies simple consequence. And therefore it sometimes affirms a consequence absolutely, but at other times indeed as things are now.

Regarding the third question, it is objected that the word "without" *(quin)* is a composite of the word "that" *(qui)* and of the adverb "not" *(non)*. Hence it is a composite of a noun and an adverb. Therefore it ought to be a noun or an adverb, since every word derives its signification from its possible components. It must be said that this word "without" is a simple [word], as I believe, having consecution from its comprehension along with negation from the nature of its imposition. Because it is generally said that it is a composite of the word "that" *(qui)* and the adverb "not," one must therefore answer differently in supporting the positing of these. Hence one must say that the word "without" *(quin)* is a conjunction and is a composite of the indefinite noun "that" *(qui)* and the adverb "not." For composite conjunctions have diverse and varied compositions. For some are composed of other conjunctions, for example, "and" *(et)*, "but" *(at)*, "and also" *(atque)*, "and indeed" *(etenim)*, "if indeed" *(siquidem)*, and others of the same sort. Others, indeed, are composed of pronouns, as "on account of this" *(ideo)*. Still others are composed of nouns and prepositions, as "on account of that" *(quapropter)*. Yet others are composed of several nouns and a preposition, as "for that reason" *(quamobrem)*. Others, indeed, from several verbs: "As one can see" *(videlicet)*, "as one can know" *(scilicet)*. Still others are from an elective *(electivo)* adverb, for example, "yet" *(quamquam)*. Others are from an adverb and a verb, as "as much as you please" *(quamvis)*. And Priscian[33] seems to indicate this in his larger work in the treatise *"On the Conjunction"* determining concerning the species or concerning the function of the conjunction. For nouns or pronouns or prepositions or adverbs are met with which are understood in lieu of causal conjunctions. Now to the objection that a composite word materially derives its signification from its components and that the word "without" will be a noun or an adverb, one must answer that it does not follow that it is a noun or an adverb because of the fact that a composite word materially derives its signification from its components. For sometimes one composite comprehension in the same genus arises from the partial comprehensions of the components, as for example, "magnanimous," "omnipotent." At other times, however, the components are of diverse genera and the composite remains in the genus of one of them, for example, "any one that" *(quisquam)*; for this is a (pro-)noun composed of a (pro-)noun and a conjunction. Again, at other times, the composite word is of a genus other than that of each of its components, for example, "on which account" *(quare)* is an adverb composed of two nouns. This is because sometimes one of the components is completive of the signification of the composite word, and then the composite remains in the same genus with its completive component, for example, "magnanimous," "hundredfold." Sometimes, however, the comprehension of a composite word does not arise from the partial comprehension of its components, rather it arises from the relations or

[33] *Inst. Gram.,* xvi, 1.

comparisons of the components. Hence, because these two ablatives, namely, "on which" *(qua)* and "account" *(re)*, indicate the relation of a cause from the point of view of its causality, and further, because that ablative "on which" *(qua)* is interrogative, it follows that one comprehension is constituted adverbially from these two compositions, namely, the interrogation and the causality, by a union of their ablatives; thus the interrogative "on which account" *(quare)* is constituted. In this way a composite word materially derives its signification from its components. Therefore it does not always follow that a composite word is of the same genus as its components. Similarly, I say that sometimes relation, sometimes interrogation, sometimes indefiniteness belongs to the (pro-)noun "who" *(qui)*. Hence on this account, insofar as it is an indefinite noun composed of a negating adverb or a negation, one ordered comprehension or a conjunct of several words or sentences is constituted, and thus a conjunction arises over and above the ordinative or conjunctive.

Again, with respect to the same point, a noun always affirms substance; a conjunction, however, affirms an association which belongs to the simultaneous or to that which exists according to the prior and the posterior. But this association is both of substances and of accidents, because it includes the whole field of signification, whether being or non-being. But the previously mentioned relation or association cannot follow from substance. Therefore, the word "without" *(quin)* is not a composite of the indefinite (pro-)noun "that" *(qui)* and of the adverb "not" *(non)*.

The solution, however, is clear from the foregoing, because the composition of the word "without" *(quin)*, which is derived from the indefinite (pro-)noun "that" *(qui)* and from the adverb "not" *(non)*, does not exist by virtue of a substance signified by the noun "that"; rather it exists by virtue of a union, as by virtue of the indefiniteness which belongs to the substance itself, as we said previously in the case of the adverb "on which account" *(quare)* and the like, for example, "for that reason" *(quamobrem)*, "every day" *(quotidie)*, "on the day before yesterday" *(pridie)*, "in the present circumstances" *(impraesentiarum)*, and the like. So sometimes composition arises from the significations of the components; at other times, however, it does not arise from the significations of the components, but rather from their relations.

Regarding the fourth question, it is objected that the (pro-)noun "that" signifies an indefinite substance with a subjunctive article. According to Priscian,[34] "that" *(qui)* is, among us, the same as "anything

[34] *Inst. Gram.*, xvi, 27. 3-5.

[98]

that" ($\mathring{o}$ς-τις). Among the Greeks, "that" ($\mathring{o}$ς) is a subjunctive article and "anything" (τις) is an indefinite (pro-)noun. But every article signifies a relation. Therefore, no conjunction has the nature of an article—in the second mood of the second figure. Therefore, in relation to the conjunction "without," "that" and "not" is a *non sequitur*. Therefore they are not convertible because the antecedent always posits the consequent and thus it always denotes the nature of the consequent. And one must say that "without" and "that-not" *(qui non)* are not convertible, because relative to "without" *(quin)*, "that" *(qui)* and "not" *(non)* follow but not conversely. The reason for this is because "without" affirms a consequent of an interrogation or of one negative relative to another, as for example, "He does not run without being moved." But "that-not" *(qui non)* sometimes is added to affirmatives, for example, "He is telling you that you may not come." But this is not equivalent to "without," for "He is telling you without you may come," affirms nothing. Moreover, sometimes it is added to negatives, for example, "He does not run that is not moved" and "He is not a man that is not an animal." In this second way "without" *(quin)* and "that-not" *(qui non)* are convertible and equipollent, so that if "He is not a man that is not an animal," then "He is not a man without being an animal" and conversely.

Now to the objection one must reply that the relation signified by the article is other than and different from the relation signified by the noun or by the relative pronoun, because the relation of a noun or a pronoun means that some antecedent precedes, the recollection of which is caused by the relative, as for example, "Sortes is running and he is arguing"; and thus the relative of a noun and of a pronoun are never placed at the same time with their antecedent but are naturally placed after it. But the relation of an article is of another genus because the article tends to be adjoined to the things denoted by positing a distinction with respect to the thing denoted just as syllabic adjuncts which arise by a kind of distinction in the case of pronouns, for example, "I myself" *(egomet)*, "of you yourself" *(tuimet)*. But they differ in this, because the article is not placed after the thing denoted as is the syllabic adjunct to the pronoun; nay rather the article is placed before the things denoted and one word does not arise from the article and the thing denoted as in the other case. Hence, the article is understood at the same time with the thing denoted. Therefore he asserts that the article affirms nothing about relation except in this respect, that it is understood at the same time with the thing denoted and it signifies that a kind of distinction arises with respect to the very thing itself. Because a distinction neither is nor is understood without the basis of the distinction, therefore the distinction of the thing denoted can neither be nor be understood except through the thing denoted. Hence the article indicates a relation to the very thing denoted. The relation of the article is thus one kind and the relation of the noun and of the pronoun is another. However, it is said that the article is understood simultaneously with the thing denoted. It is obvious that although we do not have such articles in the mother tongue, nevertheless we do have them in Latin, because in it the articles are always adjoined to the thing denoted. Therefore the relation implied by the article does not hinder the composition of the conjunction "without" *(quin)* nor its convertibility with the expression "that-not" *(qui non),* as we have said.

Again, a proof that the relation of the article is different from the relation of the (pro-)noun "that" insofar as it is taken relatively, because the (pro-)noun "that," insofar as it is understood indefinitely, for example, "The one that killed the tyrant, will have a reward," is not understood relatively nor does it affirm a relation to an antecedent and yet it involves the article in its comprehension. But the article affirmed a relation to the thing denoted. Therefore, the relation of the article is distinguished from the relation which is the recollection of the thing predicated. Therefore, the recollection of the article is other than and different from the relation of the noun and the pronoun. This we admit.

Regarding the fifth question it is objected and it is solved just as previously in the case of the conjunction "except," for it is always adjoined to a verb of the subjunctive mood whenever it is a consecutive word. Likewise note that the conjunction "without" or the expression "that-not," insofar as they are convertible, affirm the consecution of one negative from another negative because with respect to intention one is universally in the other of the affirmative or the affirmation of one follows from the affirmation of the other, for example, "One is not a man without being an animal. Therefore any man whatever is an animal" or "If one is a man, one is an animal. Therefore one is not a man, if he is not an animal" and "It is not a house without a wall. Therefore if a house is, a wall is." But when an affirmative follows from an affirmation, then the negation follows contrariwise, for example, "If one is a man, one is an animal. Therefore one is not a man without being an animal."

Regarding what has been said, this sophism is discussed: "You can not truly deny that you are not an ass." *The proof:* That you are not an ass is necessary. But you can not truly deny the necessary. Therefore, "You can not truly deny that you are not an ass."

To the contrary: You can not truly deny that you are not an ass.

Therefore you can not deny that you are not an ass. Therefore you are an ass.

Solution: The initial proposition is ambiguous according to those generally discussing it. For they assert that "deny" *(negare)* is equivocal in the proposition. Hence one sense is: "You can not truly etc.," that is, "You can not truly propose this negation: 'you are not an ass.'" But in this way it is false, because you can truly assert the negation: "You are not an ass." In another way the sense is: "You can not truly etc.," that is, "You can not truly propose the negation of this: 'you are not an ass,'" which is this: "It is not the case that you are not an ass," which is equivalent to this: "You are an ass." But this you can not assert truly. And thus it is true.

However, this is not a solution because denying is an act of passing from the active potency which is negative. But just as an active potency has a dual relation—one, indeed, to that from which it is or to that by which it is, namely, to the agent itself; but another to that in relation to which it is, as to the object itself into which the action passes—similarly, the act of that potency has a dual reference and also it has the same and not different references. Therefore, the act is referred to the same object as the active potency. Hence, to whatever object this potency, which is negative of it, belongs, the act of denying belongs. But that potency, which is negative, is of the predicate itself in relation to the subject. Since the negative is always a negative of something in relation to something, therefore the act itself, which consists of denying, will aways be of the predicate itself in relation to the subject. Therefore it is always of the same nature. Hence it is not equivocal. And therefore they say nothing.

Again, on the same point, just as that act, which consists of seeing, is not made equivocal by a division of blackness and whiteness, although they are opposites, similarly, denying is not made equivocal as a consequence of denying any predicate whatever, whether it shall have been the affirmed or the denied, because whether it shall have been of one kind or another, it is always removed from the subject. Therefore, denying is not made equivocal from affirming the negation: "You are not an ass," in which the predicate previously affirmed will be denied, but from affirming the negation of the proposition: "You are not an ass," in which the denied predicate is removed as follows: "It is not the case that you are not an ass." Therefore, they say nothing.

Again, on the same point, Aristotle[35] teaches us to find multiplicity in the case of inflected form and coordinates. For example, if "sanative" is affirmed in multiple ways, namely, of the causative, the preparative, and the conservative, then "to be healthy" is also affirmed in

[35] *Metaph.* iv. 2. 1003ᵃ 35.

multiple ways relative to the preparative and the conservative and so forth; and conversely, if "to be healthy" is affirmed in multiple ways and "sanative" is affirmed in multiple ways of the same things, then if one of the cases is not affirmed in multiple ways neither is the remaining—from the destruction of the consequent. But the negative is not affirmed in multiple ways. Therefore neither is "deny"—by a topical argument from inflected forms.

Again, on the same point, the proposition may be taken in accordance with the second sense which they posit. In this sense the proof and the disproof still remain. This we admit, affirming that the aforementioned proposition is no proposition. Hence we say that the initial proposition is absolutely true and the conclusion immediately following is ambiguous due to a fallacy of amphiboly, namely, the proposition: "You can not deny that you are not an ass," by reason of the fact that the verb "deny" has a construction with different relations to that which follows, namely, "that you are not an ass." For that which I affirm: "that you are not an ass," can be the object to which the "denying" itself passes and the sense is: "You can not deny truly that necessary: 'that you are not an ass.'" Thus it is true. In another way it is construed with the verb "deny," not in the nature of an object but in the nature of an end, and then the sense is: "You can not truly deny etc.," that is, "You can not truly deny anything on account of the fact that you are not an ass." Thus it is false, because if you deny that you are irrational or a brute, it follows from this "that you are not an ass." Thus there is in this case amphiboly from a diversity of construing one with another.

But to the argument that follows, namely: "You can not truly deny that you are not an ass. Therefore you can not deny without you be an ass," it can be said that it is a *non sequitur* because "without" and "that-not" are not convertible, as was said above, except insofar as they indicate the negative consecution of one thing from another. But I believe that the conclusion, in the second place, was made ambiguous, namely, "You can not truly deny without you be an ass," just as the previously mentioned was and with the same ambiguity. Hence, according as "without" and "that not" affirm consecution and are convertible from the point of view of an end, it then rightly follows: "You can not truly deny that you are not an ass; therefore without you be an ass; therefore you are an ass." But these assertions are false, as was said, and from the false the true validly follows. But it does not follow from the first proposition in this way, as explained. If, however, the construction be made from the point of view of an object, then those two inferred conclusions are true, as was said before, just as is the initial proposition also. But the last argument does not hold, namely:

"You can not truly deny without you be an ass. Therefore you are an ass." In this way there is no relation in that case, just as there is none here: "You can not truly deny that a man is not an ass. Therefore man is an ass," but rather the opposite as follows: "Man is not an ass." And similarly in the proposed, because, just as "man is not an ass," it is the object of "deny" itself in that sense. Hence there ought to follow the opposite of that which is inferred, as follows: "Therefore you are not an ass."

Again, the first proof is false, because this is true: "You can not truly state that you are an ass. Therefore you can not truly deny you are an ass"—arguing from the genus, because "to state truly" is common to "to affirm truly" and to "to deny truly." But if "you can not truly deny that you are an ass," then "you can truly deny its opposite," namely, "you are not an ass." Therefore this is true: "You can truly deny you are an ass." Therefore its contradictory is false, namely, this: "You can not truly deny that you are not an ass." But this is the initial proposition. Hence, the initial proposition is false.

Solution: The initial proposition is absolutely true. But its reasoning errs in the case of the first inference nor is there in that case a topical argument from the genus because although "to assert" is common to "to affirm truly" and to "to deny truly," nevertheless "to assert truly that you are an ass" is not general, because "to assert that you are an ass" is "to affirm" due to the fact that "to assert" is contracted by the object. Hence just as this is no argument: "You can not truly affirm that you are an ass. Therefore you can not truly deny the same," neither is there in this case any appearance of inferring in this way because the opposite ought to be inferred. Similarly in the proposed there is no argument nor any appearance of inference in this: "You can not truly state you are an ass. Therefore you can not truly deny that you are an ass."

However, it is said that "to state" is contracted by the object to "to affirm." This is clear because an act is contracted in a twofold manner: for in one way it is contracted by *differentiae* understood from the point of view of the agent; in another way by *differentiae* understood from the point of view of the object. For example, to sense by sight is the same as to see; to sense by taste is, indeed, the same as to taste; to sense by hearing is certainly the same as to hear and so forth. Hence, an act is contracted by *differentiae* understood from the point of view of the agent. But it is contracted on the part of the object as follows: to perceive a colored surface is the same as to see; to perceive a sound is, indeed, the same as to hear, and so forth. Therefore, an act is contracted from the point of view of the object. Therefore, every act having an object is contracted in a twofold manner, as

[103]

was said. Hence "to state" is said to be contracted in a twofold manner, because to state affirmatively is the same as to affirm and to state negatively is the same as to deny; and these *differentiae* exist from the point of view of the agent. Likewise, "to state that man is an animal" is to affirm it, and "to state that man is not a stone" is the same as to deny it. In this case a contradiction is produced from the point of view of the object.

Regarding what has been said, the following sophism is discussed: "At no time is something true without it be necessary." *The proof:* At no time is "God exists" true without it be necessary. Therefore the initial proposition is true.

To the contrary: At no time is "God exists" true without it be necessary. Therefore at any time whatever something is true and it is necessary. Therefore at any time that "you are seated" is true, it is also necessary.

Solution: The initial proposition is absolutely false, because the sense is: "At no time is something true, if it is not necessary." But this is false because the antecedent does not follow from the consequent due to the fact that the negation of a genus does not follow from the negation of a species. But necessity is a species of truth. Moreover, the proof errs according to a fallacy of the consequent because it validly follows: "At no time is 'God exists' true without it be necessary" and conversely "If 'God exists' is not necessary, at no time is it true." Hence the proposition which is originally assumed is true, namely: "At no time is 'God exists' true without it be necessary." For in that the truth is convertible with its own necessity. But in the others, truth and necessity are not convertible; rather truth belongs to many more than necessity. Hence there is not in this case a fallacy of the consequent in denying from the inferior to the superior, just as in this case: "At no time does man exist without he be risible. Therefore at no time does an animal exist without he be risible."

We now discuss the word "much" *(quanto)*. When we get rid of the uncertainties which surround the word "much," we must see its multiplicity. One must know that the word "much" is sometimes understood interrogatively, for example, "How much have you progressed today," to which one replies "much" or "too little" according to one's knowledge of those things; sometimes it is understood relatively, for example, "As much as I progressed in reading today, by that much you did the same"; sometimes, it is understood indefinitely, for example, "As much as you will wish, that much shall I progress." But here we consider the word "much" in none of these three modes. Now the word "much" in another way affirms a cause, for example, "By as much as the heat is more intense, by that much it produces greater warmth."

Note therefore that the word "much" sometimes affirms an efficient cause, as in the aforementioned example. For heat is the efficient cause of making warm, as "More intense heat produces more intense warmth." Again, it sometimes affirms a material cause, for example, "By as much as the body becomes more quickly organic, by so much the more quickly it belongs to the soul." At still other times it affirms a formal cause, as for example, "By as much as the soul is more quickly infused, by so much is the organic body more quickly perfected." For the rational soul originates by infusion. For it is infused by creation and it is created by infusion. Furthermore, it sometimes affirms a final cause, as for example, "By as much as the reward is greater, by so much will the labor be borne more easily."

With regard to what has been said, the following sophism is discussed: "By as much more as you learn in addition, by so much do you know less." *The proof:* Posit that you learn two statements in addition, as "Man is an animal" and "Something is," and you already know one, as "Man is a grammarian." Then one argues as follows: "By as much as that which you learn in addition is more than that which you know, by so much is that which you know less than that which you learn in addition. Therefore by as much more as you learn in addition, by so much do you know less."

To the contrary: By as much as you learn in addition, by so much more is knowledge increased in you—through a topical argument from an efficient cause. But by as much more as knowledge is increased in you, by so much more do you know. Therefore you do not know less.

Solution: The initial proposition is absolutely false, because the word "much" signifies in the initial proposition that to learn more in addition is the efficient cause of knowing less. This is impossible since it is the proximate efficient cause of its opposite, namely, of knowing more. For the same proximate cause cannot be the cause of opposites, although the remote can be, as is clear in the second book of the *Physics;*[36] just as the sailor is the remote efficient cause of the safety of the ship and of its destruction, but the sailor by his presence is also the proximate efficient cause of the safety of the ship and by his absence is the cause of its destruction, so the disproof holds validly. But the proof errs according to a fallacy of figure of speech in proceeding from one species of the predicament of relation to another species of the same category. For "greater" and "less" affirm relations caused by quantities; and, indeed, "more" and "less" affirm relations caused by qualities. Hence just as a fallacy of figure of speech arises from changing the mode of quantity into the mode of quality, or "how great" or "how many" into "what kind" or conversely, similarly a

[36] *Physica* ii. 3. 195^a 11-14.

fallacy of figure of speech arises from proceeding from a relation caused by quantity to a relation caused by quality and conversely.

With regard to what has been said, the following sophism is discussed: "By as much as anything is greater, by so much does it seem to be from the more remote. But by as much as it seems to be from the more remote, by so much does it seem to be less. Therefore, from the beginning "by as much as anything seems to be greater, by so much does it seem to be less."

To the contrary: In this case what is not the cause is signified to be the cause of the predicate. Therefore the proposition is impossible.

Solution: The initial proposition is absolutely false. For to be more is not the cause of one's seeing less, nor is it even the cause of there being less to be seen. For with respect to seeing it and with respect to its being seen, sight is required as a capacity and a colored surface is required as the object and brightness of the object or the illumination of the object is required and a medium that is air or water is required. For we see through the medium air and through the medium water. And along with these an appropriate distance is required, because, if there be no distance, the visible is not seen; for example, if the visible is placed on top of the vision or on top of the eye, or certainly if the distance were the maximum, the thing would not be able to be seen. Therefore an appropriate distance is required. The simultaneous aggregates are the efficient cause of the seeing and of the being seen. For with regard to the visual capacity, we assume an organ or an instrument of seeing. Hence, the hand is not the cause of seeing nor of being seen.

With regard to answering the proof by a destructive argument, it is said that the following is false: "By as much as anything is greater, by so much does it seem less than the more remote." For, as is said in the book *De Visu*,[37] each thing has spatial dimension due to which fact it will be seen as greater, that is, each visible thing is capable of being extended to so great a size, beyond that which is proper to it by circumstances, that if it were placed at this distance, it would not seem to be greater in size. Hence this is false: "By as much as anything is greater, by so much does it seem less than the more remote."

Many questions surround the word "than *or* as" (*quam*). The first concerns its distinction. The second, how does the word "than" imply comparison? Third, what does that comparison involve in relation to a noun [i.e., adjective] in the comparative degree? Fourth, what does the comparison involve in relation to the following nominative, for example, "Sortes is stronger than Plato." Fifth, why does the nominative follow whenever this word is conjoined to a comparative? Sixth,

[37] Non inveni.

why is the comparative sometimes construed with the ablative, at other times with the nominative, "than" having been interposed?

Regarding the first question, note that the word "as" is sometimes an adverb of similitude, for example, "He assumed this, as it were, declaring it beforehand" and "Both this one as well as that one is running"; sometimes it is an adverb of comparison, for example: "Sortes is stronger than Plato"; sometimes it is an adverb of admiration, for example, "as lucky as brilliant"; sometimes it is an adverb of indignation, as for example, "as foul a deed as unmanly a deed." In addition, this is an elective conjunction, which is defined by Priscian[38] as follows: an elective conjunction exists "whenever different things having been proposed we declare that we choose some one of them, for example, 'I prefer to be an evil rich man rather than a pauper.'" Wealth and property having been presupposed, one chooses to be wealthy, relinquishing the other. And similarly in this case: "It is good to trust in the Lord rather than etc.," the conjunction "than" is the elective conjunction. Thus the multiple usage of this word "than or as" is clear.

Regarding the second question, note that five things are required in the case of a comparison: one is that which is compared; another is that in relation to which there is a comparison or that in relation to which the comparison exists; a third is an excess in that in relation to which the comparison exists; a fourth is that to which it is compared; a fifth is the median respect between that which is compared or between that which is compared and that to which it is compared. For example, when I say "Sortes is stronger than Plato," Sortes is that which is compared; and "stronger" asserts the quality of fortitude in relation to which the comparison exists and also an excess of fortitude itself because Sortes has fortitude and he has it in excess with respect to Plato; indeed, Plato is that which is compared and the adverb "than" asserts the median respect between that which is compared and that to which the comparison is made. Hence the adverb "than" has nothing to do with the comparison save as an asserted respect. Note also that sometimes a sixth requirement is posited in the case of a comparison, that which is the measure of the excess itself. Then the comparative degree is construed with a double ablative, as for example, "Sortes is taller by one foot compared to Plato"; thus we say that Sortes is the one exceeding or that which is compared: or it is construed with an ablative and a nominative when "than" has been interposed, for example, "Sortes is taller than Plato by one foot"; and thus we say that Sortes is the one exceeding or that which is compared. And the comparative "taller" asserts that in which he exceeds and it

38 *Inst. Gram.*, xvi, 9. 25-26.

also asserts the excess of the tallness itself. And "Plato" asserts that which is exceeded or that to which he [i.e., Sortes] is compared. And the adverb "than" asserts an excess, as we said, between the exceeded and that which exceeds or that to which it is compared. And the ablative "by one foot" affirms how much an excess of tallness there is in Sortes in relation to Plato and so it affirms the measure of the excess itself. Hence as often as we want to signify the measure of an excess through a comparison, the aforementioned six things are required for the comparison. But as often as we want to signify a comparison without a measure of the excess, the aforementioned five requirements suffice. It is clear therefore that the adverb "than" introduces a comparison insofar as it asserts the median respect between the exceeded thing which is compared and that which exceeds comparatively, as we said.

Regarding the third question, note that this adverb "than" has the nature of a term with a following nominative related to the comparison, because everything compared affirms an excess with respect to some term or with respect to that which is exceeded. But the nominative cannot be the term of that excess when the adverb "than" mediates.

Regarding the fourth question, note that the adverb "than" is that through whose nature the nominative terminates the reference of the comparative because the nominative as such cannot determine the reference of the comparative. Hence it has the nature of a term through the adverb "than" and the nature of the nominative insofar as the nominative is the term of the comparative. Thus it is compared to the nominative itself as to its nature insofar as it terminates the reference of the comparative etc.

Regarding the fifth question, note that any substance is understood as active in the nominative, but in the oblique cases it is understood as passive, because the nominative affirms the active mode, whereas the oblique cases affirm the passive mode. Because the word "than" causes that which is exceeded to be referred to another act and the act is always in some agent or by something which has the mode of an agent—but the mode of the agent is in the nominative, as we said— therefore whenever the adverb "than" is adjoined to a comparative, it is proper that there a nominative follows which is compared to its act, for example, "Sortes is stronger than Plato," that is, "than Plato is."

Regarding the sixth question, note that that which is exceeded by the comparative can be signified in two ways. For in one way it is signified only insofar as it is exceeded; in another way insofar as it is exceeded and also is ordered to another act. If, however, it is understood only insofar as it is the thing exceeded in relation to the comparative itself or by means of the comparative itself, then it retains the nature of that from which the excess which is signified by the comparative is removed. For the excess is in the comparative itself with respect to the thing exceeded. It is not in the thing exceeded but rather is removed from it. Thus the thing exceeded retains the nature of that from which something is removed. But that comparison which belongs to the term from which (*a quo*), is only found in the ablative. Therefore, whenever only the thing exceeded is signified, then it is proper that it be placed in the ablative. Therefore the comparative in this mode is construed with the ablative. Furthermore, whenever the thing exceeded is signified only insofar as it is the exceeded, then it is proper that it be placed in the ablative. Therefore, the comparative in this mode is always construed with the ablative. But whenever the thing exceeded is signified insofar as it is exceeded and insofar as it is compared to another act so that it is a part of the other act, because the comparison to another act goes beyond the first comparison, namely, insofar as it is the exceeded, then the comparison to another act is as it were completive of the first comparison and therefore orders the thing exceeded relative to the other act. And because the act, as we said, is from something which stands in the active mode, therefore the nominative follows. In this way a nominative is always construed with a nominative when "than" has been interposed. And it is clear why the comparative is sometimes construed with the ablative, at other times with the nominative when "than" has been interposed. It is also clear when the comparative ought to be construed with one and when with the other. Further, it is clear that comparatives ought to be construed with a double ablative and also with one ablative and with a nominative when "than" has been interposed.

Regarding what has been said, this sophism is discussed: "It is impossible for you to know more than you know." *The proof:* This is impossible: "You know more than you know." Therefore the assertion of it is impossible. Therefore this is true: "It is impossible for you to know more than you know."

To the contrary: You can learn more in addition. Therefore you can know more than you know. Therefore this is false: "It is impossible for you to know more than you know."

Solution: The initial proposition is ambiguous by virtue of the fact that "possible" asserts a relation, because every potency of those things which are is "to something" [i.e., relative *ad aliquid*] according to Aristotle.[39] Similarly, "impossible" asserts a relation, because impotence deprives something of potency with respect to something, just as "possible" posits potency in something with respect to something, for it posits potency with respect to the initial act or with respect to the

[39] *Metaph.* v. 12. 1019ᵃ 15.

complete form or with respect to an accidental act or with respect to a comparison starting from the form itself, because to act belongs to the form. I say, therefore, that the initial proposition is ambiguous by virtue of the fact that the word "impossible" can posit its relation within the accidents, and thus the initial proposition is false and the sense is: "You cannot know more than you know"; or it can posit its action over the statement as a whole, in which way the initial proposition is true and the sense is: "For you to know more than you know is impossible," because at no time do you know more than you know at that time.

This sophism is discussed: "It is impossible that other than an ass has begotten you." *The proof:* That man be an ass is impossible. But it is other than an ass that has begotten you. Therefore it is impossible that other than an ass has begotten you.

To the contrary: It is impossible that other than an ass has begotten you. Therefore an ass begot you.

Solution: The initial proposition is ambiguous by virtue of the fact that the relative of diversity, "other," can be referred to the term "ass," and in this way the relative "other" is in the accusative case and the sense is: "It is impossible that some thing distinct from an ass has begotten you"; and in this way it is false: or the relative "other" can be referred to the statement as a whole, namely, "an ass has begotten you," then the relative "other" is in the nominative case, and the sense is, "It is impossible that other than an ass has begotten you," that is, "An other is impossible than this impossible, which is that 'an ass has begotten you,'" for example: "man is a stone" is another impossible distinct from this impossible, namely: "an ass has begotten you"; and thus it is true.

We now discuss the word "whatever" *(quicquid)*. Because the word "whatever" in one mode implies distribution, it ought on account of itself to be determined among distributions. But as far as this is concerned, that it introduces consecution along with disjunction, it ought on account of itself to be determined amongst the syncategorematic words. Regarding the word "whatever," one asks in the first place what does it signify; second, whether it is an equivocal word or not; third, whether it implies a relation or not.

Regarding the first question, note that four things are involved in the understanding of the word "whatever" or in its signification. One is distribution. Another, indeed, is the matter of its distribution, because just as the word "any thing you will" *(quodlibet)* has in itself distribution and the thing distributed by its distribution, so also does "whatever." A third, moreover, is consecution. A fourth, indeed, is disjunction. For when one says "Whatever runs, is moved," the sense is:

"Either this runs or it is not moved." Thus in this case there is a consequence and disjunction. So there are four things involved in the signification of the word "whatever."

Regarding the second question, note that although different things are understood in the signification of the word "whatever," nevertheless it is not an equivocal word because it signifies those many univocally by virtue of the fact that it signifies distribution in its subject or in the thing distributed. On account of this, when consecution occurs, it always represents one word which is the antecedent and another which is the consequent, for example, "Whatever runs, is moved."

Regarding the third question, note and it is objected that the sense of the proposition: "Whatever runs, is moved," is this: "Everything which runs, is moved." But this is a relation. Therefore the initial proposition is a relation. Therefore, the word "whatever" introduces relation. But it must be said that the word "whatever" does not introduce relation. Moreover, it is not a relative word but an indefinite (pro-)noun and a distributive sign, just as we said. It is composed by the duplication of the (pro-)noun "what" (quid), according as the (pro-)noun "what" (quid) is absolutely indefinite but not according as it is interrogative and also relative. The proof, moreover, errs according to the fallacy of accident. It is not proper, if a relation is understood in one of the convertibles, that it also be understood in the other. Hence, these two propositions are convertible: "A white man is running" and "A man who is white is running"; in one a relation is understood, but in the other a relation is not understood.

Regarding what has been said, the following sophism is discussed: "Whatever God has known, He knows." *The proof:* God knows everything and He has forgotten nothing. Therefore, whatever God has known, He knows.

To the contrary: Whatever God has known, He knows. But He has known that you are (esse) or are (fore) about to be born. Therefore He knows that you are or are about to be born. Therefore, you are about to be born.

Solution: The initial proposition is absolutely true, for the knowledge of the First Cause is always the same nor does He admit of any change in Himself. Hence God has in Himself immutable knowledge of all things. The cause of this is that He, as knower, knows according to His own mode and according to the power of His own cognition and not according to the mode of the known or of the thing known; for the cognitive power is not dependent on things but rather things depend on it as on its cause. Our knowledge, however, depends on the things known and is perfected by them, that is, our knowledge is mutable in accordance with the mutation of things; but the knowledge of the First

Cause is not mutable in accordance with the mutation of things. Now the disproof errs by a fallacy of figure of speech in changing from one predicament to another, because *substance (quid)* is changed into *time (quando)*. But the distribution "whatever" affirms *substance,* whereas "about to be born" affirms *time.* Thus *substance* is changed to *time* by the assumption of "about to be born" under *substance.* And in this case there is a sophism of accident because *substance* and *time* can be taken in a twofold manner. In one way, insofar as they are signified through language. And the predication occurs in them according to a fallacy of language on account of the motive principle. Thus *substance* is erroneous linguistically. In the other way *substance* and *time* can be taken from the point of view of the thing or as they are modes of things, language having been circumscribed. Thus the error in them produces a fallacy of accident on account of the motive principle in the thing. For I say universally, therefore, that, whenever there is a fallacy of figure of speech, there is always a fallacy of accident, but not vice versa. And this is due to diverse causes, as we have mentioned, because the modes of predicable things are diverse. If, moreover, they be taken as they are signified through words, then there is a fallacy of figure of speech. If, however, these modes are taken from the point of view of the thing, or they are modes of things, then a fallacy of accident is produced in them. Because in the first way the motive principle exists in language, but in the second way in the thing.

We now discuss the mode of questioning. An answer always follows a question in discourse, because a question is a request for an answer and it proceeds from the questioner as from an efficient cause. Because a question is understood by an answer and an answer by a question as by its cause, it must be known that a person who questions properly ought to do five things. The first is to discover the means of proof from which it be proved or by which one ought to argue. The second is to form the questions or to effect propositions expressing the means of proof discovered previously. The third is to relate these to each other. The fourth is to refer them to another as to a respondent. The fifth is that he force the respondent himself to affirm improbables. Hence, if you want to oppose well, it is necessary that you go through the five steps mentioned previously or at least the first four of them. Now Aristotle determines the five elements in the eighth book of the *Topics,* the fourth as a matter of fact at the beginning of the eighth book, the fifth in the chapter concerning an answer.[40]

It follows that now we ought to see the modes of solution in general. Now, of solutions, some are correct, others apparent. But an ap-

[40] *Topica* viii. 1. 155^b 4 sqq.; viii. 4. 159^a 18-21.

parent solution, as a matter of fact, happens in many ways. For one solution is related to the question only, for example, when an opponent is prevented from proceeding to his conclusion, although he may have a true reason. Another solution is related to time, as for example, when the solution which is given to a proposition, needs to be demonstrated by an investigation and it needs to be demonstrated in time that the proposition itself is the worst of all solutions. Each of these solutions is said to be *ad hominem*. But a correct solution is said to be a solution to the proposition *(ad orationem)*. And it is thus defined in the second book of the *Sophistical Refutations*.[41] A correct solution is the demonstration of the false and why *(propter quid)* it is false.

But there are two species or parts of a correct solution because either it exists by a destruction or by a distinction. A solution by a destruction exists whenever some one of the premises is destroyed on account of its falsity. A solution by a distinction, however, exists whenever it is demonstrated that a conclusion does not follow from the premises on account of some fallacy dependent on language or independent of language. Hence a solution by a destruction ought to be used for a proposition which proceeds from false premises. A solution by a distinction, however, ought to be used for a proposition erring according to some fallacy dependent on language or independent of language. Hence, whenever you want to solve any proposition in the case of sophisms or in other cases, consider in the first place whether it be true or false, since, if it would be false, it can only be proven sophistically. And with regard to a disproof, it must be solved by a distinction or be proven by a fallacy and then, with regard to the proof itself, it must be solved by a destruction. But a disproof necessarily ought to be true. However, if a conclusion be true, then the proof ought to be correct. But if the disproof errs according to some fallacy, then it must be solved by a distinction. If, however, it be accepted as a consequent of a false premise, then it must be solved by destruction.

The following is a division of syllogisms from the point of view of conclusions, quality, and quantity. Having spoken about syncategorematic words and having considered the things which are required of opposition in general and having seen the modes of solutions in general, we must as a consequence discuss the divisions of syllogisms from the point of view of the conclusion. It must be known that with regard to syllogisms, some are universals, others particulars. Syllogisms are called universals which have a universal conclusion, as is clear in the first and in the second and in the sixth mood of the first figure, and in the first and in the second mood of the second figure. They are called

[41] *De Sophisticis Elenchis* 18. 176b 29-31.

particulars, however, which have a particular conclusion, as is clear in the rest of the syllogisms in all the figures.

Note that universals always syllogize many or have many conclusions, because they have their proper conclusion and they also conclude to the converse of their conclusion and in addition they conclude to the particular of the proper conclusion. Besides these conclusions, moreover, universal negative syllogisms conclude to a fourth conclusion. This is the particular of the converse of its proper conclusion. For example, the second mood of the first figure implies its proper conclusion, as: "No animal is a stone. Every man is an animal. Therefore no man is a stone." And it concludes to the particular of its proper conclusion, as: "Therefore, some man is not a stone." And it concludes to the converse of its proper conclusion, as: "Therefore, no stone is a man." And these four conclusions follow from the two premises posited in the aforementioned syllogism. And just as all the universal negative moods have four conclusions, so the universal affirmative moods have three conclusions, namely, the proper universal conclusion and its particular and its converse. Hence, note that the fifth mood of the first figure is contained under the first mood because it concludes to nothing else but the converse of the conclusion. For the same reason the seventh mood is contained under the third mood because it concludes nothing else but the converse of the conclusion of the third. Hence, understand that Aristotle[42] did not separate the fifth mood from the first mood nor the sixth mood from the second mood nor the seventh mood from the third mood but Boethius[43] did. Whence Aristotle in the book of the *Prior Analytics*,[44] in determining the generation of syllogisms, does not make mention of three syllogisms, namely, of the fifth, sixth, and seventh. Rather he only says in the beginning of the second book of the *Prior Analytics*[45] that all universal syllogisms always syllogize many, that is, several conclusions, as we said. And from this Boethius[46] drew these forth.

In like manner, of particular syllogisms, affirmatives have several conclusions because each has its proper conclusion and the converse of it. Therefore, just as we said, the seventh mood of the first figure is contained under the third mood. But particular negatives have only one conclusion due to the fact that a particular negative is not convertible.

Having seen the division of syllogisms from the point of view of the conclusion as far as quantity and quality are concerned in the preceding lesson, but not as far as the principles of syllogisms—mood

---

[42] *Anal. prior.* i. 7. 29ᵃ 25-27. 29.

[43] *De Syllogismo Categorico* ii. (PL 64, 814C).

[44] *Anal. prior.* i. 4-7. 25ᵇ, 27-29ᵃ

[45] *Anal. prior.* ii. 1. 53ᵃ 5.

[46] *De Syllogismo Categorico* ii. (PL 64, 814CD).

[114]

and figure—are concerned, because the division of syllogisms from the point of view of moods and figures is contained in the treatise on syllogisms assigning three figures and their proper moods, consequently we must say that every syllogism is demonstrated in two ways, for it is demonstrated by converting and leading to the impossible or by a converse syllogism and a syllogism concluding to the impossible. One must note that the terms and the propositions in a converse syllogism and in syllogisms concluding to the impossible are arranged in the same way. But they differ in two ways. The first difference consists in this, that a converse syllogism arises from another syllogism, previously constructed, by taking the opposite of the conclusion with one of the premises to the destruction of the other premise, namely, sometimes the major, sometimes the minor. For example, if I were to accept the opposite of a conclusion with the minor, it destroys the major, for example, "Every animal is a substance. Every man is an animal. Therefore every man is a substance." The opposite of the conclusion is this: "Some man is not a substance." From this, therefore, with the minor, it is possible to destroy the major by syllogizing as follows in the fifth mood of the third figure: "Some man is not a substance. Every man is an animal. Therefore, some animal is not a substance," and this conclusion contradicts the major of the other syllogism. But if the opposite of the conclusion were accepted with the major, it destroys the minor by syllogizing in the fourth mood of the second figure as follows: "Every animal is a substance. Some man is not a substance. Therefore some man is not an animal," and this conclusion destroys the minor of the first syllogism. In this way a converse syllogism arises from the other syllogism which was previously constructed. But in syllogizing to the impossible it is not necessary to construct another syllogism first, but only some false proposition having been taken, then derive from it some more inadmissable proposition which is known to be false. Hence, if the opposite of the false will be demonstrably true and on account of this destroys the false proposition which was previously assumed, then it is said to be a syllogism concluding to the impossible (ad impossibile); for example, if you grant this proposition, namely, that "Trees do not have a soul" and from this you conclude to the more impossible false "Therefore trees are not nourished nor do they grow'." But this is impossible. Therefore it is impossible that "Trees do not have a soul." In this way a syllogism concluding to the impossible (ad impossibile) has been constructed. The second difference is that a converse syllogism exists for to show that an inference is necessary. But a syllogism concluding to the impossible (ad impossibile) exists to show that a proposition is false. Consequently, it exists to show that the opposite of the proposed itself is true. It must be known that

[115]

any syllogism whatever of any figure whatever can be demonstrated by its own figure or an inference and by a converse syllogism, as we have said. And also any conclusion whatever of any syllogism whatever can be demonstrated as regards its truth by a syllogism concluding to the impossible, as was said. But if anyone should want to be quick in these, it is necessary that he frequently be exercised in such syllogisms. These statements of Peter of Spain concerning syncategormetic words are sufficient.

Treatise on Obligations

In the second book of the *Ethics*,[1] the renowned leader of the philosophers, Aristotle, says that art and virtue are concerned with the difficult. Moreover, he significantly mentions two things briefly which by their difficulty customarily entrap beginners in a terrible fashion. The first is stated in the first book of the *Prior Analytics*[2] and in the ninth book of the *Metaphysics*,[3] namely, "the possible having been assumed to belong, nothing impossible follows." The second is stated in the fourth book of the *Metaphysics*[4] concerning a certain special, and as it were, anomalous kind of propositions which destroy themselves by their own signification, because from the being so as they represent by direct signification, they are falsified by a certain reflection. Wherefore the paternal solicitude of the author has led him to discuss briefly the art by which beginners are instructed in responding and opposing in two *opuscula*, namely the *Treatise on Obligations* and the *Treatise on Insolubles*. They are valuable for breaking out of traps and for firmly entrapping the unskilled. So putting our hand to the aforementioned treatises by first beginning the treatment of obligations, it remains first to set down the descriptions of certain terms, secondly to add some necessary rules, then in the third place finally to add the practice of a few examples for the sake of a fuller exposition.

As far as the first is concerned a description of obligation is offered which is given by some as follows: An obligation is the premising of something assertible in order to maintain it in some state, namely, affirmative, negative, or dubitative. It can also be described in another way: An obligation is the premising of some assertible possible in order to maintain it lest the impossible follow. This description agrees with the proposition of Aristotle in the first book of the *Prior Analytics*,[5] which is that "the possible having been conceded or admitted, nothing impossible follows," although this often happens in descending in accordance with the triple state. One must note that just as there is no perfect premising unless the concession of the respondent intervenes, so an obligation does not properly exist unless the respondent admits what is premised. For if the opponent says: "I posit this to you: 'Every man is in Rome,'" an obligation is not assumed until the respondent says: "I admit." By this act there is as it were a sort of eager request for controversy between an opponent and a respondent. And that is the role of an obligation, to the maintenance of which within the time of the obligation the respondent himself is restricted by his concession.

[1] *Nichomachaean Ethics* ii. 3. 1105ᵃ 9.
[2] *Analytica priora* i. 13. 32ᵃ 16-30.
[3] *Metaphysicae* ix. 4. 1047ᵇ 10.
[4] *Metaph.* iv. 8. 1012ᵇ 14.
[5] *Anal. prior.* i. 13. 32ᵃ 19-20.

Or a second description is devoted to the obligate itself as follows: The obligate is the proposition immediately following the sign of obligation which enjoys the role of an obligation only for as long as it is still admitted. Example: Let the opponent say: "I posit this proposition to you: 'Every man is in Rome,'" then: "Every man is in Rome" is the obligate, because it follows the expression "I posit this to you," which is called a sign of obligation. Or if one were to say: "I ask you to concede the first thing proposed to you by me," then the complex expression "to concede the first thing proposed" follows a sign of obligation, namely, "I ask," and therefore it is called the obligate. Moreover, the signs of obligation are: "I posit," "let it be posited," "I ask" and the like, or also their opposites, as for example, "I reject," etc.

A third description: The period of time of an obligation is that which follows as a logical consequence of the concession of the respondent until the opponent says: "Let the time of the obligation end" or he obliges the respondent in a way contrary to the way of the primary obligation.

A fourth description: The relevant to any proposition is that which follows from it or is repugnant to it. For example, if this be admitted: "Sortes is seated," then relevant to it is: "Sortes is not running," because it follows from it. Similarly this proposition: "Sortes is standing or Sortes is not seated," because it is repugnant to that. There is therefore a twofold relevancy, namely, the sequent and the repugnant. And because that last proposition is repugnant to the proposition which it follows, the term relevant is extended to it. Therefore, although a multiple subdivision of the relevants can be ascribed, nevertheless in this art the relevant is only concerned with that which is called a sequent from the obligate only or from the obligates by a valid concession or from valid concessions or from the opposite of a valid denial or valid denials. For example, if one were to say: "I posit this to you: 'Every man is in Rome,'" and the respondent were to admit it, then: "You are obliged," is relevant to the act of the respondent, because it follows as a logical consequence of the aforementioned act. In like manner the proposition: "Something was proposed to you," is relevant in this way, because it follows as a logical consequence of the act of the opponent. But such relevants are irrelevant to this art. Rather the propositions: "You are in Rome" or "It is not the case that you are a man" and the like are called relevant propositions according to this art. This is obvious in the syllogistic process involved in arguing as follows: "Every man is in Rome; you are not in Rome; therefore, you are not a man," or as follows: "Every man is in Rome; you are a man; therefore, you are in Rome."

Next follow the rules. The first rule is: "The possible having been assumed to belong, nothing impossible follows"; also "That which has been posited absolutely *(simpliciter)*, must be admitted universally." The first part of the rule is made clear by Aristotle in the places previously mentioned,[6] wherefore one must pay attention to the fact that a *differentia* is usually assigned between a proposition "concerned with the possible" *(de possibili)* and a possible proposition. For a proposition "concerned with the possible" is called a modal proposition when it is modified by the mode "possible" without a negation destroying it, for example: "It is possible that Sortes runs." But if it were destroyed by a negation, then it ought rather to be said to be "concerned with the impossible," for example, "It is not possible that white be black," that is, "it is impossible." But a possible proposition is said to be one which is such that whatever is signified by it in the sentence as a propositional whole, to such an extent it is possible to be, taking the term "to be" generally, as in the case of someone citing some true proposition, whether affirmative or negative, we say that it is so. From this it is usually inferred that any proposition is "concerned with the possible" *(de possibili)* which is not possible and contrariwise. For the following proposition is "concerned with the possible": "It is possible that every man is an ass." Yet it is impossible and contrariwise. For this proposition: "Every man is an animal" is possible and yet it is not "concerned with the possible."

According to the aforementioned distinction, there is a twofold exposition of the statement in which it is said: "The possible having been assumed to belong, nothing impossible follows." [It is explained] in one way, obviously, as follows: If a possible proposition is cited and it is assumed to belong, that is, if it is conceded to be actually so in reality as the proposition itself signifies, nothing impossible follows, although the false can follow. It is explained in another way as follows: The possible having been assumed to belong, that is, a true proposition "concerned with the possible" having been cited and it is assumed to belong, that is, if it be correctly assumed in relation to one concerning the present, the impossible does not follow. "True" is asserted significantly, because a false proposition "concerned with the possible" is impossible. Therefore it is not inadmissible if the proposition, which is itself categorical *(de inesse)*,[7] is impossible, for example, "It is possible that man is an ass." Similarly one did not vainly state "if it be correctly assumed to belong," for if "incorrectly" were stated, then the impossible could happen.

Whence some modifications are usually expounded, insofar as the positing to belong can be made correctly. The first is that if a universal sign or one including it is posited in a proposition "concerned with

---

[6] Cf. n. 2 and n. 3 *supra.*   [7] Literally "concerned with belonging."

[119]

the possible," then in place of such a sign its singulars ought to be understood conjointly. But it suffices that any one whatever of these particularly can be true, for example, if one were to say: "A line can be divided into all proportional parts," "Lines can be divided into infinite parts," it is posited categorically as follows: "A line is divided into these proportional parts" and "A line is divided into these" etc., but not as follows: "A line is divided into all proportional parts."

A second case of modification is that if in the proposition "concerned with the possible," the predicate of the statement is referred to the material content of the subject in such a way that a *sensus divisus* follows, then by positing that in one of the present tense the material content itself or its equivalent ought to be understood, for example, "It is possible that white be black," that is, "This subject is black," "Sortes can walk without feet"—whatever is signified by this proposition thus is possible to be.

A third modification follows: if any determination which is repugnant to a copula in the present tense is posited, then it ought to be omitted in positing the proposition in one with the present tense, for example: "It is possible that Sortes is running tomorrow," for this is incorrect: "Sortes is running tomorrow."

The second part of the rule follows from the first part, for to the person responding validly the impossible does not follow without exception from the possible. It remains that it should be conceded, every possible must be admitted absolutely. However to those to whom it seems otherwise, a more accurate reaction will come later.

The second rule is as follows: All our responses and the oppositions made at the time of the obligation ought to be considered as made for the same measure of time or the present. And one must respond to everything irrelevant in the same way, as if an obligation should never have been made. The first part of the rule is obvious. For if not so, someone could admit two contradictories. The second part of the rule is made clear by an example, as, let the proposition "You are in Rome" have been posited and admitted, then let it be posited that "Some man is a Parisian." Because it is irrelevant and true, it must be conceded. For to everything irrelevant one must make the same response within the time just as outside the time, namely, according to the quality of its signification.

The third rule: Just as mutually contradictory propositions must never be conceded or denied within the same time of an obligation, so every proposition, having once been admitted by the respondent according to some status, must always within the time of the obligation, as often as it is proposed, be maintained in the same status. This is obvious, because all responses are regarded as having been made adequately for the same measure of time, and so contradictories cannot be conceded. Hence a proposition, once conceded, always ought to be conceded within the same time of an obligation, as often as and in whatever place it shall have been proposed. For if not, then its contradictory would be conceded.

The fourth rule: Every sequent from a valid concession or valid concessions or from the opposite of a valid denial or valid denials or from everything simultaneous within the time of the obligation, must always be conceded. This is obvious, because if not, then it would be necessary for the opposite to be conceded, and this is inadmissible. Similarly, the repugnant to the aforementioned or to any of the aforementioned must be denied according to the sense prescribed.

The fifth rule: It is not improper that the respondent might admit within the time of the obligation that he concedes the false or that he responds invalidly. But if, the time of the obligation ending, he is forced to concede that he has responded invalidly within the time, then he has been led to the goal of disproof. The first part is obvious, because everything possible is admitted in this art. But from some possibles it follows that he can admit that he concedes the false and that he responds invalidly, as will be revealed later in practice. Therefore. The second part is obvious, because outside the time one must respond in accordance with reality. If therefore he is then forced to concede that he has responded invalidly within the time, what was proposed is obvious.

The sixth rule is: Any proposition proposed within the very time of the obligation in regard to one place is relevant and must be conceded, and this proposition, if it would have been proposed in relation to another place, would be denied. It is obvious from an example, as this proposition having been posited and admitted "Every man is in Rome," let it be proposed; also the proposition: "You are a man," ought to be conceded, because it is true and irrelevant; then the proposition "You are in Rome," must be conceded, because it is a sequent from the validly conceded obligate. But if this, "You are in Rome," would have been proposed in the second place and this, "You are a man," in the third place, then each of the two would have to have been denied, because the first is false and irrelevant, the second is repugnant to the proposed validly denied.

The seventh rule is: One must always respond to everything absolutely necessary or impossible with an exactly similar response. This is obvious from its opposite. For just as the possible must be admitted and that proposed under the form of the posited must be conceded, so the absolutely impossible must never be admitted but rather it must always be denied and the absolutely necessary must always be admitted. Moreover, "absolutely" *(simpliciter)* is asserted of the necessary and the impossible, because something is called necessary or impossible essentially *(secundum quid)*, though to be sure, on account of a lapse of time, any such propositions as "You have been in Rome," [and] "You have not been in a colony," can sometimes be true and sometimes false. But nevertheless after you have been in Rome, for the rest of time the propositions "You have not been in Rome," cannot become true. Therefore, these are the chief and more general muniments of this art, by the study of which the studious beginner can repel any spears whatever thrown at him. Next, some minor principles shall be able to be touched upon in the exemplary practice of this art as opportunity will provide. Consequently, examples follow for a fuller exposition of what has been said previously.

Let an opponent say to a respondent: "I posit this to you: 'One of two *(alter)* of them is an ass,' must be admitted, if it is possible." Then let the opponent say: "I propose to you that the same propositions must be conceded, because anything, once admitted, must be conceded whenever it is proposed, as the third rule states." Next, let this be proposed: "'One *(unus)* of them is an ass' must be conceded according to the second rule, because it is true and irrelevant." Then let this be proposed: "One of two *(alter)* of them is an ass." If you concede, it is argued against you: "The following is a logical consequence: 'One *(unus)* of them is an ass; and one of two *(alter)* of them is an ass; therefore each *(uterque)* of them is an ass'; but this is impossible; therefore it was invalidly conceded." If you deny, it is argued against you that the proposition itself was validly admitted and conceded and consequently it must be conceded whenever it is proposed. The response is that the proposition itself is not being proposed, having been repeated in a similar sense or form, as it was from the beginning, having been posited, admitted and first conceded, because in the first place the term "one" *(alter)* was understood indefinitely but in the second place it was understood relatively. But this way one is not proceeding according to the intent of the rule.

A second example. I posit this to you: "'Every man is in Rome' must be admitted, because it is possible." Then let the opponent say: "I propose to you that the same must be conceded, because, having been admitted validly once, it is proposed under the same form." Then this is proposed: "You are not obligated." If you deny it, the proposition itself is irrelevant and must be conceded outside the time of the obligation. Therefore, it must be conceded within the time of the obligation. The consequence holds by virtue of the second part of the second rule. If you concede, *contra:* the proposition itself is irrelevant and false, because the positing and the admission have obligated you.

The response. One must deny that the rule is understood, other things being equal, because then this proposition varies as to truth and falsity prior to the obligation and subsequently. Hence it is that the intent of the rule is not obstructed in responding to it in a different way within the time of the obligation and outside the obligation, just as it is responded differently to the proposition: "Sortes runs," when he is running and when he is at rest.

A third example. Let this be posited to you: " 'You are not speaking,' must be admitted, since it is possible." Then if it is proposed, it must be conceded. Then let this be proposed to you: "You are conceding something." If you concede this, it follows that "You are speaking." The response. The posited must be admitted. Then the proposed must be conceded. Then when this is proposed: "You are conceding something," it must be denied. But when it is developed, it follows that: "If you deny something, it is true that 'you are speaking.' " But when it is said "You have denied that you conceded something," it is denied, although according to what is really true it may be so. Nevertheless, it must be denied because of repugnancy to the obligate. For it is not inadmissible to deny one's own act, if the obligation requires it.

A fourth example exactly similar to the aforementioned is the following. Let it be posited that a is a predicate of some proposition. When this has been admitted and conceded, let this be proposed to you: "No a is a predicate." This having been conceded, let this be proposed to you: "No predicate is a." If you concede this, you are conceding a proposition in which a is predicated. But thus you are granting the opposite of that which was posited. If you deny this, it is argued against you as follows: "Certainly the following is a valid inference: 'No a is a predicate; therefore no predicate is a.' But the antecedent has been conceded. Therefore the consequent must be conceded." The response is that: "No a is a predicate" is converted into this: "No predicate is a"; and that the consequence: "No a is a predicate; therefore no predicate is a," must be conceded, whenever it will have been proposed; and that one concedes the proposition: "No a is a predicate," if it will have been proposed. Thus one is bound to concede this proposition: "No predicate is a." And in relation to the instance in which it is insisted that if you concede it, you are conceding a proposition in which a is predicated, the respondent ought to assert that he does not concede this: "You are conceding it," namely, the proposition which is the consequent. Yet he ought to concede the consequent whenever it is proposed to him. In like manner he also ought to concede the whole conversion proposed but yet deny that he concedes it. For it is one thing to concede some proposition which is proposed to someone and it is another thing to concede that he concedes it. For the proposition and the concession of the proposition are considered irrelevantly. And thus, as before, it happens that the respondent is bound within the time of the obligation to deny his own act.

A fifth example. Let it be posited that the following propositions are mutually convertible: "God is" and "Man is an ass." This having been admitted, because it is possible, let the same be proposed, it will have to be conceded. Then let this be proposed: "God is." It must be conceded, because one must always respond in the same way to everything necessary. This having been conceded, let this be proposed: "Man is an ass." It must be denied, because it is impossible. But on the contrary, everything necessary must be conceded. But this: "Man is an ass," is convertible with this, namely, "God is," which is necessary. Therefore, it must be conceded. Hence the respondent invalidly denies it.

Or, in another way, when the posited has been admitted, let this be proposed: "God is; therefore man is an ass." If you concede, *contra:* one must respond to every consequence in the same way within the time and outside; but it is denied outside the time; therefore also within the time. If you deny, *contra:* every consequence in which one argues from the convertible to the convertible is valid and must be conceded; but one is arguing in this case from the convertible to the convertible; therefore it was an invalid denial.

Or that which was first posited can be made more definite as follows, namely, let it be posited that the following are mutually convertible: "God is" and "Man is an ass," signifying precisely that God is. But then let the reason be advanced as a consequence that it was set forth as a premise. In considering a response to those previously mentioned positings, in which the matter of the positing is taken in some way or other, one must note that, although the respondent ought to maintain the positings made at the time of the obligation, nevertheless they are not true positings as far as the real truth is concerned. No, for if I were to say "I posit that this: 'Man is an ass,' means that God is," then it is truly the case that its signification is changed. And to the extent that there is similarity to them, one must respond as if no positing would have been made. Also the rule is ascribed that everything posited is irrelevant to its own positing. For example, when Sortes is running and Plato is arguing, if one were to say "I posit that these are convertible or that they have the same signification, namely, 'Sortes is seated' and 'Plato is arguing.'" This having been admitted, if this be posited: "Sortes is seated," it must be denied, because it is false and irrelevant. Again, if one were to say "Man is a dissyllabic word," "Man runs," the term "man" is accepted in the first proposition

[124]

in a way different than in the second. For in the first proposition a predicate which belongs to the word as such is posited and it implies a reception of the word whereas in the second proposition it is accepted for the external reality which is signified by the word. In a similar way, while "God is" and "Man is an ass" are affirmed as such, they are convertible or they have the same signification. Also, similarly, while one states that "God is" and "Man is an ass," such propositions are not understood in the same way. For in the first way they are accepted as it were for themselves and propositional properties which can properly belong to them are attributed to them. But in the other case they are posited absolutely and are accepted for the realities themselves.

Hence, these things being kept in memory, one easily responds to many things previously read. For example, let it be posited that the following are convertible and have the same signification: "God is" and "Man is an ass." Let the respondent admit this. And if it be proposed, let him concede it. Also let him concede this: "God is," whenever and wherever it is proposed. Contrariwise, he ought to deny that "Man is an ass" wherever and whenever it is proposed. Also he ought to deny this: "God is; therefore man is an ass." Then, going further, every consequence, whose antecedent and consequent are truly convertible and have precisely the same signification, is valid and must be conceded. But in such a consequence as "God is; therefore man is an ass," the antecedent and the consequent are truly convertible and have precisely the same signification. This minor is absolutely false, as is obvious from the first statement of this example. Nevertheless, the respondent has to admit that on account of the obligation. Therefore he has to concede the minor. When an inference is made, it must be conceded. Behold! it is possible to concede that it must be conceded. And if a further inference should be made and you do not concede it, then you are responding invalidly. Certainly it is possible to concede this as relevant, that one can respond validly in accordance with what is really true, when one is proceeding according to the rules of this art. Nor is this inadmissible, as a man at some time or other is bound to deny his own act—a man who can in the proposed case use a similar mode of responding, so that if an inference is made, the consequence must be conceded—it seems acceptable thereafter, that when an inferior is inferred and you do not concede it, it is possible to deny one's own act, even though it may be that the denial of one's own act more frequently happens by virtue of a contingent obligation. Therefore, it is very profitable to pay attention to this when one is arguing from an acceptance for the reception of the word to an acceptance for the external things, for which reason it is not necessary that the argument

[125]

prevail. For if it be said "The time of the obligation is ended," then you have responded invalidly within the time. The respondent ought to deny this, for he is responding validly and relevantly. Nevertheless he can concede that he conceded outside the time that he responded invalidly within the time, for this was a relevant sequent. But if one were to say "You have denied a consequence whose antecedent and consequent were truly convertible," it is obvious from what has been said above that they were not truly convertible. But now, freed from the obligation, he ought to deny that. Thus it appears that he has responded validly within the time.

Certainly it is customary apparently to be very persistent against the aforementioned, especially because the admitted proposition, namely, "Man is an ass" is convertible with the proposition "God is." There is a contrary argument. For this: "Man is an ass," necessarily signifies that man is an ass, so that it cannot signify differently. Therefore it was invalidly admitted that it could be converted with this: "God is." A valid consequence is supposed. Also the antecedent is proved. For grant the opposite, that it can signify that man is an animal, then it follows in the first place that it would not signify in accordance with the imposition of its terms. The consequence is obvious, because its terms are "man" and "ass." If, therefore, it would not signify that man is an ass, it seems that it does not signify according to its terms and the signification of the terms. But this is inadmissable because the signification of the whole results from the signification of the parts. Then in the second place the following is a logical conclusion, because when the imposition is reverted to, this: "Man is an ass," is true, just as this: "Man is an animal," is now true, for their extremes are the same; therefore, just as it is true to say that "Man is an animal" signifies that man is an animal, so with respect to the other it will be true to say that it signifies that man is an ass.

One responds to these instances by maintaining what was treated previously. Hence one must deny that this: "Man is an ass," cannot signify otherwise than that man is an ass. And with regard to the proof, when it is said: "If it can signify otherwise, then it would not signify according to the imposition of its terms," one responds by simply denying the consequences. Nevertheless it must be conceded that it can signify, not by signifying according to this imposition of its terms which it now has and which is constantly objectively referred to the determinate realities which are a man and an ass. But if it is then inferred that it would not signify according to the signification or imposition of its terms, one would be arguing from the inferior taken negatively to the superior taken negatively. To the second instance one responds by conceding that, the imposition of the terms having been adverted to, this: "Man is an ass," is true, and one denies the consequence in which it is said: "Therefore, just as this: 'Man is an animal,' signifies that man is an animal, so this: 'Man is an ass,' will signify that man is an ass." The reason for this is that the aforementioned accusatives stand for the very realities which are a man and an ass. But when it is said: "This is true: 'Man is an ass,'" the aforementioned nominatives are not accepted determinately for the very same realities which are a man and an ass but either for the words themselves or generally for some signified things with respect to which there happens to be a conformity of the thing understood to the intellect. But if in accordance with what is really true, "An animal is an ass," they would have the same signification from the primary imposition, just as the words *"Tullius Marcus"* and *"Cicero"* signify the same man synonymously. This being so according to what is really true, then just as it is true that the two propositions "Tullius is a man," "Marcus is a man," signify that Cicero is a man, similarly, the two propositions "Man is an animal" and "Man is an ass" should be conceded to have the same signification. Also this: "Man is an ass" should, after a true imposition, signify that a man is an animal. In this way nothing inadmissable follows.

A sixth example. Let the term *a* be imposed to signify only as much as "every man" does and *b* as much as "animal" does. This having been admitted, the proposition: "A is *b*," is proposed. If it is denied, *contra*: "Every man is an animal; therefore *a* is *b*." The consequence holds, because the antecedent and the consequent have the same signification. If it is conceded, *contra*: "No *b* is *a*; therefore *a* is not *b*." The consequence holds and the antecedent is obvious, because "No animal is every man; therefore no *b* is *a*." The consequence holds from an equivalent to an equivalent. The response to this example is made in different ways by different people. Some admit the posited in accordance with a law of this art. Then they deny this, if it is proposed: "A is *b*," because the irrelevant and that which is outside the time should be denied. And with regard to the proof when it is said: "'Every man is an animal; therefore *a* is *b*.' The consequence holds from an equivalent to an equivalent," the consequence is denied but it is conceded that they are equivalent. Yet in another way the one obliged has to concede this by virtue of the obligation, even though it may be otherwise according to what is really true. And if the last inference is made, you deny the consequence in which the argument is from an equivalent to an equivalent, then you are responding invalidly. It is obvious from what has been said previously, that it is not inadmissable that the respondent can admit that he has responded invalidly within the time, when some obligation demands that. However, others have customarily responded differently but validly, because they pay no attention to the law of the art of the obligatory nor do they assume the role of one who is obliged. Rather, as it were, the real truth would be such that a and "every man" would have the same signification, likewise b and "animal." Then they concede that "A is b" ought not to be converted so. For a universal sign and a general term is involved in its subject. Therefore in the first case it ought to be resolved just as this: "No one is an ass." Thus this: "A is b," ought not to be converted simply, because it is a universal affirmative and therefore ought to be converted *per accidens*. Thus in the first case it should be resolved into this: "Every man is b" and this is converted as follows: "Therefore some b is a" etc., because "No animal is every man." In a similar way, "A is something" but yet "Nothing is a," because "Every man is something" and yet "Nothing is every man." By this line of reasoning in exactly the same way, that "A sees b" but yet that "B should not be seen by a" are conceded. For example, the primary imposition remaining and along with this that "Every man sees himself and no other animal," then "A sees b," because "Every man sees some animal," but yet "B is not seen by a," because it is false that "Some animal is seen by every man," and so forth analagously in the case of things with the same foundation. It does not seem that this line of thought should be regarded lightly, because in accordance with now this and now that consideration it is not inadmissable to vary responses, now in one way and again in another way.

A seventh example. Let the term a be imposed in a true proposition to signify "ass," in a false proposition to signify "man," and in a doubtful proposition to signify the complex expression: "man or an other than man." Then let this be proposed to you: "Man is a." If you concede and even though it be irrelevant, it is true. Thus it signifies "ass" and so in conceding "Man is a," you are then conceding that man is an ass. If you deny, then it will be false, even though it is irrelevant. And so a signifies "man" and consequently you deny that a man is a man. If you doubt, then you doubt this: "A man is a man," or what is not doubtful, "an other than man."

There is a controversy among famous men concerning this mode of obliging by imposition. For Buridan does not admit of such a genus of obligation and he assigns a reason, because the constitution of a proposition presupposes that words have already been imposed for signifying but this mode of obliging presupposes conversely that the proposition has been constituted and is true or false and then signification comes to a word by imposition, and so there is a repugnancy in this kind of positing. On the other hand, Marsilius universally and absolutely allows such impositions in accordance with the principle of

this art, namely, that everything which can be posited [i.e., the pos-
able], if it should be posited, must be admitted. A middle way can be
chosen by a sound better judgment. It is definite that this kind of imposition represents that the imposition of the word happens at the same
time with the constitution of the proposition although truth or falsity
is naturally presupposed in the proposition. But there are some impositions where the repugnance is clearly apparent. Just as if one were
to say: "Let the term '*a*' be imposed in the proposition: 'Man is *a*';
if it be false to signify 'man' and if it be true to signify 'ass' etc."

Still "to coincide" and "to match" are similarly related. For example, if one were to say: "The one running is *a*," it can be posited
to anyone in such a way that *a* signifies "man," if it is false, and "ass,"
if it is true. Nor do those who distinguish in this way want to avoid
the practice of this art. Rather they want to show the circumstances of
imposition and of obligation. Hence, the posited having been admitted,
universally whenever this: "Man is *a*," is proposed, it is denied,
because the irrelevant and that which is outside the time should be
denied. When one says "if it is false," then it signifies "man" and consequently in denying this: "Man is ," you are denying that man is man.
This last consequence is denied, just as in similar circumstances it
was asserted above that this: "Man is an ass," is conceded to be convertible with this: "God is." But nevertheless whenever it is proposed,
the one itself is conceded and the other is denied. In a similar way,
there is a controversy among the authors mentioned with regard to a
certain other mode of obligation, namely, of dependency. For example,
if one were to say "I ask you to concede the first thing which I propose
to you," then an impossible proposition can be the first thing proposed. Therefore Buridan says that such an obligation must not be
allowed, because sometimes it refers to the impossible. Marsilius, on
the contrary, indifferently allows it. But then if "Man is an ass," is
proposed first, he denies it. Then when one insists: "You ought to
concede the first thing which I propose to you; but the proposition:
'Man is an ass,' is the first thing proposed; therefore you must concede
it," the response is that it must be conceded. Consequently someone
can concede that he responds invalidly. Nevertheless, the respondent
would respond better to that in terms of the same form, affirming: "I
admit what must be admitted; I deny what must be denied; and I
doubt what must be doubted."

An eighth example is one in which the incomplex is posited to
signify complexly. For let it be posited that *a* should signify adequately only as much as the statement: "God is." This having been
admitted, let *a* be proposed to you. If you concede, although it may
be irrelevant and outside the time, it should not be conceded that you

are responding invalidly. If you deny or doubt, then you deny or doubt the proposition: "God is." Again let *a* signify one of these: "God is" and "Man is an ass." And you not knowing that the truth of the matter is that it signifies the proposition: "God is," then let this: "A is true," be proposed. If you concede, it is argued as follows: "A is true; but *a* is doubtfully: 'Man is an ass'; therefore this: 'Man is an ass,' is true." If you doubt, it is insisted as follows: "You know this: 'God is,' is true; but *a* is this: 'God is'; therefore you know *a* is true; therefore you do not doubt that '*a* is true.'" Some respond to the first of these, not according to the practice of this art, nor under the form of an obligation, rather they would have it according to what is true. Hence, the posited having been admitted, they concede *a*, if it is proposed to them. A simile of this was touched upon in the seventh example. Others respond according to the precepts of this art. For, the posited having been admitted, when *a* is proposed, neither do they concede it, nor deny it, nor doubt it. Because it is irrelevant and outside the time, neither should it be conceded nor denied nor doubted. But if it be said that: "A is a true proposition which is convertible with this: 'God is,' since this follows from what was posited by you," then you ought to concede it. The response is obvious from the similes frequently mentioned above. Certainly it is conceded that *a* should be conceded. But yet whenever it is proposed, neither is it conceded, nor denied, nor doubted. With regard to the second, one answers by doubting each of the two accepted by itself, although copulatively, there is no doubt. Then when it is said: "You know this: 'God is,' is true; but *a* is this: 'God is,'" one answers that that is doubtful. Then if it be inferred that: "therefore you know *a* is true," one responds that it is not inadmissable that a thing be known in one way and unknown in another, because "knowing" is spoken of in many ways, namely, either in relation to itself or its own form, or in relation to its principles, or as the remotely known according as it is accustomed to be determined elsewhere. Others speak otherwise in relation to this and they say that this ought to be distinguished in a composite and a divided sense. Certainly, if it is composite, it must thus be denied, because it is only valid insofar as you know this composition or proposition: "A is true," and this is false. But if it is divided, it is true, and the meaning is: "You know *a* is true," that is, "You know that that which is *a* is true." But thus the proposition is true, because "that which is *a*" is the proposition: "God is," by virtue of the case posited, and you know that this is true. In this way many propositions can be saved, for example, this: "You know that some proposition is true which no man knows is true"; and similarly if you doubt that this proposition is true; also similarly: "You know that every truth is true."

A ninth example. Let the truth of the matter be that you are seated. And let this proposition be posited to you: "You are in Rome." This having been admitted, let this: "You are in Rome and you are seated," be proposed to you. If you deny, then you deny your copulative, each part of which must be conceded by you, namely, the first, because posited, the second, because true and irrelevant. Certainly, if you deny, this is proposed to you: "You are seated." The argument is the same, if you doubt. If you concede, *contra:* "You are not in Rome or you are not seated; if you are in Rome, then you are not seated." The consequence from a disjunctive whole with the destruction of one part to its other part is valid. And the minor is the posited. But if you concede or doubt the first copulative, you are conceding or doubting a false and irrelevant proposition which is known to be such. Note that in this case some deny that this is false: "You are in Rome and you are seated." Because you are seated here, it follows that the proposition: "You are seated" is true, as is obvious from Aristotle who says in the Postpredicaments[8] that the fact of the being of a man is convertible with the proposition which asserts that a man is. Also this: "You are in Rome," is conceded. Therefore it follows that the copulative is true, because the truth of the copulative demands that each part be a true one and an irrelevant one which is known to be such. It is responded to, after admitting the posited, by denying the copulative, namely, this: "You are in Rome and you are seated." When it is said that "You are denying a copulative, each part of which must be conceded," this must be denied as soon as the copulative in the second place will have been proposed. For then this: "You are seated," although it may be true, nevertheless is a repugnant relevant proposition, as was deduced, so that, if this: "You are seated," would have been proposed in the second place and the copulative in the third place, then both would be conceded, namely, the first, because true and irrelevant, and the copulative as a relevant sequent from the conceded. But now according to the other order, each must be denied. This agrees with one principle of this art mentioned previously, that the same proposition according to one order and position has one status and in another situation has another status, as is certainly obvious in the case of the following example. When you are not dwelling in the holy estate, let this be posited to you: "Every man is in Rome." This having been admitted, if this: "You are a man," is proposed in the second place, it must be conceded. Then this: "You are in Rome," must be conceded. But if each would have been proposed in the other order, certainly each would have been denied.

A tenth example. Let this be posited to you: "The proposition:

[8] *Metaph.* ii. 11. 993[b] 30.

'Man is an ass' has been posited to you and has been admitted by you."
Or I posit this to you as follows: "It must be admitted that: 'Man is
an ass' must be conceded by you." Then let this be proposed: "'Man
is an ass,' must be denied, because it is absolutely impossible." But
contra: "Everything posited to you and admitted by you must be conceded by you; but this: 'Man is an ass,' has been posited to you and
admitted by you; therefore it must be conceded." I concede that it
must be conceded. And when it is argued further: "You are not conceding it; therefore you are responding invalidly," I concede that I am
responding invalidly, not because it is true, but because it follows. Or
as follows: "This proposition: 'Man is an ass,' must be conceded; but
you are not conceding it; therefore, you are responding invalidly." The
response is that the posited proposed under the form of the posited
must always be conceded within the very time of the obligation. But
it does not happen this way in the case of what has been proposed.
For it is posited as a part of some whole and as conjoined with something additional. Then afterwards it is proposed particularly according
to a different acceptation of the terms. Similarly, if, when you are
seated, this is posited: "This is true: 'You are standing.'" This having
been admitted, let this be proposed: "You are standing." It must be
denied in this case because it is false and irrelevant. But *contra:* "This
is true and irrelevant: 'You are standing'; therefore it is invalidly denied." The response is that I concede this whole: "This is true: 'You
are standing,'" to be true as posited, but I deny the proposition: "You
are standing," when it is taken by itself. But if it is demonstrated in
this way, then it is neither true nor relevant. Still it is customary to
posit the following. When you are seated, let this be posited to you:
"As soon as 'You are standing' is proposed to you, the proposition
must be denied by you." This having been admitted, let this be proposed: "'You are standing' must be conceded, because it has been
posited and admitted." Then let this be proposed: "You are not standing." If you concede, then you are conceding two contradictories
within the very time of the obligation. If you deny, then you are denying the true and irrelevant. The response is that if this: "You are
standing," is posited absolutely, then its opposite must always be
denied. And it is denied because the obligate is not involved, for an
apposed condition does not become a part of the obligate. But if it
should be a part of the obligate, then this: "You are standing," is irrelevant to the obligate and false, and consequently must be destroyed.

An eleventh example. Let this be posited to you: "'Only God is
God' is posited to you." This having been admitted, let this be proposed to you: "'God is God' is posited." This, it seems, must be conceded, because it follows from the posited, just as the prejacent fol-

lows its exclusive. But on the contrary, if you concede, it does not follow that: "'God is God' is posited to you." Rather "God is God" differs from "Only God is God." Therefore, it is not the case that: "'Only God is God' is posited to you." This is the opposite of the posited.

In like manner, when the posited has been admitted, let this be proposed: "'Nothing other than God is God' is posited to you." When this has been conceded because it follows from the posited, let this be proposed: "'An other than God is God' is posited to you." This, it seems, must be denied, because it contradicts the conceded. If, therefore, you deny, it is objected *contra:* "This is posited to you in the demonstration of the proposition: "'Only God is God' is posited to you"; but this is the case that 'An other than God is God'; therefore. . . ." One responds to the admitted according as the term "only" is taken exclusively, so that the sense is: "The proposition: 'God is God,' is posited to you and no other." But if the term "only" is taken materially in this case, it must not be admitted in this way, as its sense is: "This exclusive proposition: 'Only God is God,' is posited to you," having been posited in the conceding of the proposition: "'God is God' is posited to you," if only the term "only" performs the function of an exclusive with regard to the following statement and it is held dividely. And when one argues: "'God is God' is posited to you; but 'God is God' is other than 'only God is God'; therefore it is not the case that '*Only God is God*' is posited to you"; it is obvious that in the minor premise the term "only" makes the sense composite and consequently it is not considered as exclusive and a fallacy of composition and division is committed by virtue of this. Therefore.

A twelfth example. If, God foreknowing from eternity the antichrist to be about to be, it is still possible for the antichrist not to be about to be, then let it be posited to belong, namely: "The antichrist will not be." It seems to follow that the knowledge of God is not necessarily fulfilled or that the contingency of future events cannot stand along with His foreknowledge. The response is that the above statement equipollently contains two positeds and one sublates the other, for example, if one were to say: "I posit that God foreknows the antichrist to be about to be born," which must be admitted as true. Then let this be proposed: "The antichrist will be born." This is a true and relevant sequent. Then let this be proposed: "It is possible for the antichrist not to come into being." This is likewise conceded. And it is acceptable when one says: "Let it be posited to belong." But this positing "to belong" sublates the other, namely, that in which one posits "to foreknow the antichrist to be about to be." Similarly, if one were to say: "Everyone predestined will be saved" or "It is necessary that the predestined be saved" and "It is possible not to be saved," if it is posited as belonging that "He would not be saved." The response is that such a positing destroys the hidden prior positing in which it is signified the predestined to be about to be; therefore, etc.

Thus, in conclusion, readers have learned that the doctrine of this treatise, whose principles no science can certify, can be practiced according to these principles. Nevertheless, the rules upon which it rests are contained in what was treated previously. In fact, a few examples have been added in order that handguiding may uncover for beginners some new examples for consideration and for practicing on both sides so as to uphold any possible whatever, like those knowing the trap of the hunter. This was the intention of the author in approaching this art under the guidance of the Most High, who is blessed forever and ever.

Treatise on Insolubles

Because every promise falls due in the case of a pledge, freed now from the one I had stated with respect to what must be said concerning the art of obligation and its practice, the second promise remains, namely, to add a few things concerning the propositions which are called insolubles, additions by which keen beginners can, by the use of previous exercises, solve such insolubles and propose insolubly to the unskilled. Thus three things present themselves for explanations. The first is, what is an insoluble or what proposition can be called insoluble. Second, from which, as it were, principles does it happen that some proposition is called and becomes insoluble, and what might be the cause of the reception of this in some propositions but not in others. The third is to bring together some examples for forming and solving them, seeing that they perceive by sensible experience the mode of forming similar ones and of resolving them, if they will have been opposed by others.

So, with regard to the first thing, an insoluble proposition can be specified by a certain kind of circumlocution. An insoluble proposition is one which causes difficulty with regard to whether it ought to be called true or false because of a secondary signification which reflects on the direct signification. In this specification, "signification" is posited as a genus. Next the cause, "which causes difficulty with regard to whether it ought to be called true or false," is posited as a *differentia,* corresponding to a proposition regarding the way in which it is insoluble, because, unless there was a difficulty in discerning truth or falsity, it would not deserve to be called insoluble. Finally, one says "because of a secondary signification which reflects on the direct signification," by which an insoluble proposition differs from exponible propositions, which, it is allowed, need exposition on account of their obscurity. However, the difficulty of an exponible proposition and an insoluble one is of a different genus. Certainly, the present definition can be clarified by an example. For instance, if Sortes asserts this proposition alone: "Sortes is saying what is false," this proposition directly signifies that some statement of Sortes is false, but because he states that very proposition alone, it follows that secondarily it is turned backward on itself by its own signification and it signifies that it is false. From what is so follows what is not so. Thus from this definition a kind of *differentia* of insoluble propositions is made clear. For some immediately reflect a secondary signification on the direct signification, as is evident in the aforementioned example. However, some mediately reflect a secondary signification on the direct or primary signification, for example, if Sortes says: "Plato speaks the truth," and he says nothing else. Plato, on the contrary, asserts this alone:

[135]

"Sortes is saying what is false." This having been granted, it follows that the proposition of Sortes becomes false. But still Plato cites a true proposition, from whose signification as it were the signification of the proposition which Sortes cites is made ambiguous. For if the propostion of Plato which signifies that Sortes is saying what is false, is true, the propostion of Sortes destroys itself. Again, from an examination of the same definition, controversies between some outstanding men can be settled. Buridan[1] says that an insoluble proposition, for example, "Sortes is saying what is false"—let it be that he says precisely that and nothing else—signifies that Sortes is saying precisely what is false, and consequently it is as the proposition itself signifies but yet it is false. He wants therefore that the proposition on that account not be called true or false, because it is just as is signified by the proposition itself in its entire signification or it is not. On the other hand, Marsilius,[2] maintaining an opposite opinion, says that not only does it signify that Sortes is saying what is false but it also signifies secondarily that it is false that Sortes is saying what is false on account of a secondary signification which is repugnant to the primary signification, not directly and essentially but accidentally by virtue of the circumstance of the case; and so it is not properly said to signify that which it implies reflexly. However, by turning one's attention toward the repugnancy which arises from the direct signification and the circumstances of the case, in this way the signification of the proposition itself is generated but it is simply not the case as it is signified by it. Now this secondary response is more consonant with the Philosopher. For in the fourth book of the *Metaphysics*[3] he defines truth by the being as and falsity by the not being as is signified by the proposition.

With regard to the second thing, we must see from which principles it happens that a proposition is called and becomes insoluble, and what might be the cause of the reception of this in some propositions but not in others. But the origin of the falsifying of some proposition itself can be revealed to those paying diligent attention to Aristotle about the end of the fourth book of the *Metaphysics*[4] where he says as follows: "And so therefore it happens—and this is an often expressed view—that all such propositions destroy themselves. For he who says that everything is true, makes the contrary of his own statement true, and therefore his own not true. Then, to be sure, he who says everything is false, makes his very own statement false." For from these words we can educe that the words "true" and "false" or any other words which include them or from which they follow, such as "necessary,"

---

[1] *Sophismata Buridani* (Paris: Antoine Denidel and Nicolas de la Barre, ca. 1495-96), chap. 8, sophism 7.

[2] Non inveni.

[3] *Metaphysicae* iv. 7. 1011ᵇ 25-27.

[4] *Metaph.* iv. 8. 1012ᵇ 15-18.

"impossible," "to be deceived," "to be knowable," can cause the re-flexion of a proposition on itself and destroy the direct signification. Because the signification of a whole results from the signification of the parts, when a part of the proposition implies a certain proposi-tional attribute, it overflows as a consequence into the sentential and whole signification of the proposition, and so on account of this certain accident intervening, the proposition destroys itself. For this reason we must pay attention to the fact that the truth of a proposition consists in a kind of conformity or agreement of the thing understood and the intellect itself compounding and dividing. Therefore, if any proposition signifies that its opposite is true, it remains that the truth of the opposed proposition cannot agree with such a primary and direct signification. Hence it follows that the intellect considering such repugnancy turns back on the first proposition to destroy it.

It is immediately evident from these premises that some proposi-tions from their reflection only are false but they remain possibles, for example, this: "Sortes is saying what is false." If he says that alone, then it falsifies itself. But if he also says this "Man is an ass," then such a proposition is true. For some propositions, from their reflection, be-come impossibles, for example, if one were to say: "This is false" to indicate the proposition itself, or "This is true," to indicate its contradictory etc. Secondly, it is evident that substance, quality, and quantity are attributed to self-reflexive propositions. For example such a proposition as: "Sortes is saying what is false," is categorical, as some say, for the secondary signification is as it were adventitious and accidental, and it is affirmative and singular according to the direct signification. Opposition arises by proposing negation absolutely. It must be understood analagously in other cases. Thirdly, it is also evident that there is not a multiple proposition but rather one, be-cause both significations are involved in judging about truth or falsity. Fourthly, it is evident that propositions which are constructed of abso-lute terms which signify natural objects in the absolute are not natur-ally constituted to be self-reflexive, as "Man is an animal," "Man is risible," "Man runs."

With regard to the third thing, some examples must be added for a fuller exposition of the statements. Now some previously mentioned examples having been presupposed, let there be a different example, namely, "Every proposition is negative," or "No proposition is nega-tive," "Every proposition is particular." It remains that the genus of the stated propositions is determined by the terms, whose signification refers to a propositional attribute, but the signification of these proposi-tions reflects on them and thus there cannot be an agreement of the intellect with such a signification of the proposition.

[137]

A second example is: "God is and this copulative is false" and "Man is an ass or this disjunctive is false." In the case of these propositions and exactly similar ones the original one falsifies itself because from the being so as is signified by it is signified the not being so, as is evident to anyone paying careful attention.

A third example. Let the truth of the matter be that no man other than Sortes is deceived, although he himself believes the opposite. Then let the following consequence be formed: "Sortes believes that some man is deceived; therefore some man is deceived." It is evident that the consequence is true, because the antecedent cannot be true without the consequent being true. But *contra:* The antecedent is true as it is posited, but the consequent is false. This is proved as follows: Because no man other than Sortes is deceived and another than Sortes is deceived but Sortes is not deceived, if therefore Sortes is deceived, then he believes in accordance with what is; consequently he is not deceived. It must be said that Sortes is deceived. Also the consequence should be denied. Therefore he believes in accordance with what is, because this proposition: "Some man is deceived," to which Sortes sticks, is self-reflexive from the circumstance of the case and is equivalent to this: "Some man is assenting to a false proposition," but this cannot be true while the circumstance remains as cited. From this it is usually inferred that some propositions, as regards the signification of their parts, are wholly alike, but yet one is false because of self-reflexion and the other is true. For this proposition: "Some man is deceived," in the mind of Sortes is not true in the case posited. But if someone else should form one similar to that, such would not be false, because it would not possess the circumstance of self-reflexion. An example exactly similar to this is obvious: if Sortes says this and nothing else: "Plato is saying what is false," but contrariwise Plato says this alone: "Sortes is saying what is false," then each of the aforementioned falsifies itself. But yet if John asserts these: "Plato is saying what is false," "Sortes is saying what is false," each would be true because it has only one direct signification in accordance with which it is so as is signified.

A fourth example. Sortes knows that a proposition written on a wall is doubtful to him. It is posited that this alone is written on the wall and that Sortes looks at it thoroughly and pays diligent attention to it. Then it is argued as follows. Sortes assents to this proposition which is written on the wall. The proposition which is written on the wall is doubtful to him and consequently it is just as is signified by the proposition which is written on the wall. Consequently, since he himself is an expert, it follows that he knows that it is so as is signified, and he does not doubt. But if he does not assent, then it is not so as the proposition written on the wall signifies. But he, being an expert, knows that it is not so. Therefore it will be false. It is evident, therefore, that now the proposition is self-reflexive by the nature of the case. Hence if this proposition were to be written: "The stars are equal to one another," then the truth of the original would stand. But now it does not stand. A similar example exists if the following proposition is proposed to Plato who is most learned in every science: "This is proposed to someone, a proposition which is doubtful to him," but he does not know whether "the proposition which is doubtful to him," is proposed to someone else. Or then the proposition proposed to him will be doubtful to him. But if this is the case, since he himself is most learned, he knows that the doubtful proposition is proposed to someone and he does not doubt it. If, however, it is not doubtful to him, it will be false. Inasmuch as one can argue that he does not know whether the doubtful proposition is proposed to another, it remains therefore that it contains self-reflexion.

A fifth example is: "This negative is not known by you." Let it be posited that the very proposition itself is demonstrated and is proposed to Sortes who is skilled in every art. Then if he should know it, it will be false and consequently not known. Or he should not know it. But if he knows this and consequently knows that it is so as is signified by it, then it will be known. Therefore it remains that it is repugnant for it to be known by reflexion. Hence another case is customarily posited, namely, that every proposition known by you is affirmative. And then it is argued as follows: "Every proposition known by you is affirmative; therefore this negative is not known by you." The consequence is valid and is known to be such. Also the antecedent is known. Therefore the consequent is known. But if this is the case, the consequent will be false, and so not known. And thus it will be known and not known.

Treatise on Consequences

We are going to treat of consequences for the guidance of the young. First I shall set down what is noteworthy. Then I shall set down some rules. As far as the first is concerned, one must note that the term *"consequence"* in one way is taken in an extremely general way, namely, insofar as it is extended to both a valid consequence and to an invalid one. Then, it is defined as follows: A consequence is a statement *(oratio)* which contains more than one proposition and denotes that one of these is a sequel of the other. We accept it in this way when, any consequence having been posited invalidly, we make an affirmation by denying the consequence. In a second way, *"consequence"* is taken properly and is defined as follows: A consequence is a statement having an antecedent and its consequent as its principal parts and also a sign of an inference understood inferentially. For if the sign of an inference were not understood inferentially, but by chance materially, then it would not be a consequence; or even if the value of that sign of an inference were to be obviated by a negation, it would not be a consequence, as this proposition reveals: "It is not the case that God *is* therefore something is." But taking consequence properly only a valid consequence is called a consequence.

Note first that the antecedent is that which through the mediation of the inferential sign implies a consequent or that which antecedes another proposition in a valid consequence.

Secondly, one must note that a consequent taken properly is a proposition which is inferred from the antecedent through the mediation of an inferential sign. Also one must note that the inferential sign is a conjunction or an adverb denoting a sequel of one proposition from another.

Thirdly, one must note that to concede a consequence and a consequent is not the same. For sometimes a consequent must be conceded but a consequence must be denied, for example, it is obvious that in case that it is posited that Sortes and Plato are seated, the proposition "Plato is seated" must be conceded, but the consequence, "Sortes is seated; therefore Plato is seated," must be denied. Similarly, a consequence must sometimes be conceded, but the consequent and the antecedent must be denied, as for example in the case of the consequence: "If an ass flies, then an ass has wings."

Fourthly, one must note that the validity of a consequence requires that in no possible case can the antecedent be true without its consequent, so long as the signification of the terms remains the same. From this one infers as corollaries that it does not follow that "Every man is an animal; therefore you are an animal"; nor does it follow that "You are a man; therefore you are colored"; nor does it follow that "God is; therefore heaven is," and so forth.

Fifthly, one must note that it is not sufficient for the validity of a consequence that in no possible case can the antecedent be true without the consequent. For the following consequence is not valid: "No proposition is negative; therefore some proposition is negative." Nevertheless in no possible case can the antecedent be true without the consequent. That this is so is clear from the following, that in no possible case can the antecedent be true, the existing signification of the terms still remaining. That this is so is clear from the following, that as quickly as the proposition itself exists, "some proposition is negative," and consequently as quickly as it exists, the proposition itself is false, because the proposition itself signifies that no proposition is negative and this for that time is false. The same holds for the consequence: "Every proposition is particular; therefore some proposition is not particular" and similarly for other consequences.

Sixthly, one must note that every consequence is valid which is so circumstanced as it is asserted to be by its antecedent according to its propositional sentence as a whole and which is impossible to be without its being so as is asserted to be by its consequent according to the propositional sentence as a whole. This noteworthy point is understood with regard to consequences whose antecedents and consequents are affirmative categorical propositions in the present tense and of a categorical character. So one must speak analogously about consequences composed of different propositions.

Seventh, one must note that some divide consequence into a consequence valid as of now (ut nunc) and a consequence valid absolutely. They say that a consequence valid as of now is one which holds in itself and explicates the existence of the consequent, for example, in the case of the proposition: "Man is an animal; therefore that man is an animal," to indicate an existing man and no further by the term "that." But the following is an absolutely valid consequence according to them: "A man is; therefore an animal is." But one must note that they invalidly divide valid consequence into valid as of now and into valid absolutely, because the consequence which according to this mode is called valid as of now is not valid but invalid as is obvious from the aforementioned consequence: "Every man is an animal; therefore that man is an animal." This is an invalid consequence, for it remains in a possible case, namely, after his death, that the antecedent would be true but the consequent false.

Eighth, one must note that every consequence which is valid now, will always remain valid as long as it shall exist with the same signification of terms. Nevertheless many consequences are now valid which previously were invalid, as is obvious in the case of: "John is; therefore Aristotle was" or "Heaven is; therefore the colony was a beautiful state." These consequences are now valid and always will be valid. But they were not always valid, because, before Aristotle was, the first proposition was not valid; also, before the colony was, the second proposition was not valid. The reason why they are valid as of now is that the consequent of each is a necessary one from which a consequent of each is a proposition about the past, a true proposition whose consequent does not depend upon a future contingent. But every such proposition is a necessary one and one in relation to which one can properly call the aforementioned consequences valid and similar in nature to those as of now. Someone could say that consequences which always were and will be valid are valid absolutely. He who should use terms thus, can in a valid enough manner divide consequence into valid as of now and valid absolutely.

Ninth, one must note that valid consequence is divided into formal and material consequence. A formal consequence is one which holds in the case of all exactly similar terms, the form of arguing in exactly the same manner having been retained, so that the quality and quantity ought to be the same in the way in which non-relative general terms should be said to be exactly similar among themselves and in the understanding of grammatical relatives such as are "that one yonder" (ille), "he himself" (ipse), and the like. And I am saying something worth noting in the definition: "which holds in the case of all exactly similar terms," because there are many formal consequences which do not hold in the case of all exactly similar terms, although an exactly similar form can be held. This is obvious concerning an explicative syllogism. An example of a non sequitur is: "A man is an animal; an ass is an animal; therefore a man is an ass." It is certainly obvious in the case of such a syllogism in which the middle term is taken in the minor premise with a relative of identity, because such a mode of arguing validly prevails with a relative of identity. It is formal, but without a relative of identity it is not formal. An example of the first is where it validly follows: "A man is running; but that man is a substance; therefore a substance is running." The following is an example of the second, for it validly follows: "A man is running; but that man is a sophist; therefore a sophist is running." Secondly, I said something worth noting in the definition when I said: "the form of arguing in exactly the same manner having been retained." By this it is denoted that exactly the same quality and quantity of the propositions and exactly the same copulas of these and exactly the same position or order and number of the terms ought to exist, because these are held in the consequences from the point of view of form. But the extremes of the propositions, namely, the subjects and the predicates, and the mode of signifying of the terms themselves are understood materially. But one must pay attention to the fact that consequences of the kind which are mentioned herein ought to be called formal consequences, primarily, all syllogisms, whether they are explicative or composed of general terms; similarly every conversion of terms; similarly every argument from exponibles to the explained and conversely; similarly every argument from a whole copulative to one of its parts; similarly every argument from a whole disjunctive with the destruction of one part to the other part; similarly every argument from that from which an induction is made to the induced, when a particle is added in the antecedent, and so on; similarly every argument from the same to the same. A material consequence is one which holds on account of the matter and signification of the terms, one which is valid in the case of some terms but not in the case of all exactly similar terms, as consequences from the inferior to the superior. Similarly a consequence from this only is valid, that the antecedent is impossible and its consequent is necessary. As will be clear later, anything whatever formally follows from understanding that the impossible implies a contradiction. Similarly from the convertible to the convertible, as for example, "A man is running; therefore a risible man is running."

With regard to the second thing which I set out to do, some rules must be added, the first of which is: In the case of any valid consequence the contradictory opposite of the antecedent follows from the contradictory opposite of the consequent but the converse does not hold, that the contradictory opposite of the consequent follows from the contradictory opposite of the antecedent. To prove the first part of the rule I assume one thing which has to be proved elsewhere, that from any proposition whatever any other proposition whatever follows or its opposite stands with that. Then I prove the first part of the rule. The following should be an example and I accept the consequence: "A horse is running; therefore an animal is running." And I prove that the contradictory of the antecedent, namely, this: "No horse is running," follows from the contradictory of the consequent, namely, from this: "No animal is running," because if "No animal is running; therefore no horse is running" does not follow, then by supposition the opposite of the consequent, namely, "Some horse is running" stands along with that antecedent, "No animal is running." And also the opposite of the consequent stands along with the opposite of the antecedent, namely, "An animal is running," because it implies it in the consequence. For it follows that "A horse is running; therefore an animal is running." And the opposite of the antecedent, namely, "A

[144]

horse is running" stands along with the two contradictories, namely, "An animal is running" and "No animal is running." Consequently two contradictories stand simultaneously. But this is opposed to a first principle. The second part of the rule is obvious. Although it may follow that "A man is running; therefore an animal is running," nevertheless it does not follow that "No man is running; therefore no animal is running."

The second rule is this: In every valid consequence, if the antecedent is possible, the consequent is possible; but the contrary is not so, because sometimes the antecedent is impossible but the consequent is possible, as is obvious in the case of this consequence: "No God exists; therefore a man is running." Similarly, in the case of any valid consequence, if the antecedent is true, the consequent is true; but the contrary is not so, as is obvious in the case of the aforementioned consequence. And it is denoted in this verse: From the false, the true; from the true, nothing except the true. Similarly, in the case of any valid consequence, if the antecedent must be conceded, the consequent must be conceded; but the contrary is not so, as is obvious in the case of the aforementioned consequence.

A third rule: The entire consequence whose antecedent is impossible is valid: but if that impossible implies a contradiction, the consequence itself is formal; and if it does not imply a contradiction, the consequence itself is material. The first part of the rule is obvious from the sixth point which we said was noteworthy. The second part is proved from one. And all the others can be proved similarly. For this is a formal consequence: "Sortes is running; and Sortes is not running; therefore he is an ass." And this is proven. For the consequent follows from the antecedent by formal consequences existing between the middle terms. This is proven by arguing as follows: "Sortes is running; and Sortes is not running; therefore Sortes is running or a man is an ass." This consequence is formal, because the first part of the consequent, namely, this: "Sortes is running or a man is an ass," formally follows from that part of the antecedent, namely, "Sortes is running," because the argument is from a disjunctive part to a disjunctive whole. Similarly the second part of the consequent, namely, this: "Sortes is not running," formally follows from the second part of the antecedent, namely, "Sortes is not running," because the argument is from the same to the same. Therefore it follows that the whole consequent follows from the whole antecedent. Then from that consequent it further follows formally that "A man is an ass." In arguing in this way: "Sortes is running or a man is an ass," the consequent is formal, because the argument is from a disjunctive whole with the destruction of one part relative to the other part. Therefore from be-

[145]

ginning to end there is a valid formal consequence. And this is what was to be proved. The third part of the rule is obvious from the ninth point which we said was noteworthy. It is obvious exemplarily from this consequence: "Nothing is; therefore something is." This is a material consequence, because it does not hold in the case of all exactly similar terms, the form of arguing in exactly the same manner having been retained. For it does not follow that: "Nothing running is; therefore something running is." But you might say: "This is a material consequence; therefore something 'by which' (*quo*) is formal; therefore it is invalid to say that it is material." The antecedent is proved. Because its antecedent implies a contradiction, the consequence holds. For it validly follows that "Nothing is; therefore something is," as was admitted. Also it follows that "Nothing is; therefore nothing is," arguing from the same to the same. One answers the other argument by denying the antecedent in which it is assumed that the aforementioned consequence is formal.

As to the proof, I deny the argument, namely, that this implies a contradiction. And then the antecedent is denied. For this consequence is not a formal one: "Nothing is; therefore something is"; nor is this: "Nothing is; therefore God is."

First, it follows as a corollary from this rule that any proposition can be inferred in a valid consequence from an impossible antecedent. This is indicated when it is asserted generally that: "Anything follows from the impossible."

Secondly, it follows as a corollary that, in a valid consequence, a necessary proposition follows from any proposition. This is indicated when it is affirmed as a corollary that: "The necessary follows from anything whatever." It is obvious that in any consequence the opposite of the antecedent follows from the opposite of the consequent, for that of which the antecedent is necessary, its opposite is impossible and anything whatever follows from the impossible, as was said. Therefore the corollary is true.

The fourth rule is: It is a valid consequence from an inferior to its superior. In the case of this rule one must note that in order that one term be superior to another it is required that that term be predicated universally of the other but not contrariwise. For in positing that "No animal exists with the exception of man," "animal" is predicated universally of the term "man" and contrariwise, for in this case "Every man is an animal" and "Every animal is a man" but nevertheless it is superior.

Secondly, it must be noted in relation to this that in order that one term be superior to another it is not requisite that a consequence of a subsisting thing should not be convertible with that other. For the term "being" is superior to the term "God" but nevertheless just as it follows that "God is; therefore being is," it also follows conversely that "Being is; therefore God is."

Thirdly, it must be noted in relation to this, that in order that one term be superior to another it is requisite and sufficient that the term itself be universally and truly predicated of that other and it be inferred from that in a consequence of a subsisting thing, because that other is so related that it is not predicated of the term itself universally or it is so related that one does not conversely infer a consequence of a subsisting thing.

These things having been laid down beforehand, one argues against that fourth rule in the first place as follows—It does not follow that "You are here; therefore you are on the roof"; also it does not follow that "You are a cleric; therefore you are the pope"; and yet, as it seems, one is arguing from the inferior to the superior. The response is that in this case one is not arguing from the inferior to the superior according to the intent of the rule, because the rule is not speaking of the superior as regards place or as regards position or office of honor but as regards universality.

Second, it is argued as follows: It does not follow that "A horse is not a man; therefore a horse is not an animal," and yet one is arguing from the inferior to the superior. The response is that the rule is understood without a negation preceding the superior and the inferior.

Third, it is argued as follows: It does not follow that "Every man runs; therefore every animal runs"; here one is arguing from the inferior to the superior. The answer: This consequence is only valid undistributively and therefore it ought to be posited from the point of view of a superior and an inferior predicate.

Fourth, it is argued as follows: It does not follow that "Only a man is a man; therefore only a man is an animal," and yet one is arguing from the inferior to the superior from the point of view of the predicate. The response is that one is arguing there with the destruction of the inferior and the superior, for the predicates in these exclusive propositions stand for and denote confusedly and distributively whereas the rule is understood when one is not arguing distributively.

Fifth, it does not follow that "Sortes begins to be white; therefore he begins to be colored," and yet here one is arguing from the inferior to the superior. That it does not follow is obvious because if I posit that "Sortes begins to be white" and that "previously he was black," then the antecedent is true, namely, "Sortes begins to be white," and the consequent is false, namely, "Sortes begins to be colored," for previously he was colored, on which account he previously was black by accident. The response is that a consequence is not valid from an inferior to a superior with the words "begins" and "ceases" when they precede the inferior and the superior. The reason is because they are said to include negation. On account of this cause the following consequence is not valid: "A horse is stronger than a dog; therefore it is stronger than an animal," for the term "stronger" and any comparative whatever has the power of distributing the following general term and properly so from itself insofar as it is comparative. On account of the same cause this consequence is not valid: "A horse is as strong as a man; therefore a horse is as strong as an animal," because the term "as" also has the power of distributing, and the same holds for many other words.

Sixth, it is argued as follows: It does not follow that "If you are running, a man is running; therefore if an animal is running, then a man is running," because the antecedent is possible but the consequent is impossible; and yet one is arguing in this case from the inferior to the superior, because "animal" is superior to the term "you." The response is that it does not hold universally true in the case of hypothetical propositions.

Seventh, it is argued as follows: It does not follow that "A horse is a non-man; therefore a horse is a non-animal," and yet it seems that in this case one is arguing from the inferior to the superior; for just as the term "animal" is superior to the term "man," so it seems that the term "non-animal" is superior to the term "non-man." The response is that in this case one is not arguing from the inferior to the superior, because although "animal" may be superior to the term "man," nevertheless the term "non-animal" is not superior to the term "non-man," as is obvious to one considering the significations of the terms, because a negation added to a superior makes the superior inferior and contrariwise.

Eighth, it is argued as follows: It does not follow that "God is contingently the Creator; therefore God is contingently something." The answer is that one is arguing implicitly with a negation in this case, because the term "contingently" includes negation. For it is obvious that this: "God is contingently something," is valid only as God is able to be something and God is able not to be something.

Ninth, it is argued as follows: It does not follow that "It is doubtful whether Sortes is a man; therefore it is doubtful whether Sortes is an animal," and yet one is arguing from the inferior to the superior. That it does not follow is now proven. I think that it follows that Sortes may be seen by distant men and that it may well be known that he is an animal, but it may not be known whether he is a man or another animal. Then the antecedent is true and the consequent is false. The response is that the term "it is doubtful" virtually includes negation.

[148]

For it is obvious that to doubt a proposition is to doubt about a proposition by not asserting the same but also to hesitate or to be ignorant as to whether it is as it signifies or not.

Tenth, it is argued as follows: It does not follow that "I know a man; therefore I know an animal," and yet one is arguing from the inferior to the superior. That it does not follow is easily made clear by speaking of the appellation of the noun. For it remains that I know a man under the concept of man although I do not know an animal under the concept of animal or under the concept corresponding to the term "animal." The response is that in speaking of the appellation of the noun, as we generally speak of it, there is not a valid consequence from the inferior to the superior with words signifying the internal act of the mind, which words are said to cause an appellation of reason, as do the words "understand," "know," "choose," "wish," and similar words.

In the eleventh place it is argued as follows: It does not follow that "Risibility is a property of man; therefore risibility or crudity is a property of man," and it is false. Similarly it does not follow that "Sortes is a proper noun; therefore Sortes or Plato is a proper noun," because the antecedent is true, as is known, but it is obvious that the consequent is false, because it signifies that this composite, "Sortes or Plato," is a proper name, and this is false. The response is that the consequent must be divided, namely, the composite: "Risibility *or* crudity is a property of man." For the whole "or" is taken at the same time materially and the term "or" likewise. But then the consequence is not valid: "Risibility is a property of man; therefore risibility or crudity is a property of man." Nor is one arguing here from the inferior to the superior. But the consequent is true as also is the antecedent. But when one says that the consequent signifies this composite, "Risibility or crudity," is a property, one is denying this. But it would be validly signified as follows, if the term "as well as" *(etiam)* were taken materially. There is the same response to the second one.

In the twelfth place it is argued as follows: It does not follow that "Sortes is the lord of Henry; therefore Sortes is the substance of Henry." Similarly it does not follow that "Sortes is a zealot for justice; therefore Sortes is a something for justice." Similarly it does not follow that "Any act of Plato's depends upon an act of understanding of Sortes; therefore any act of Plato's depends upon an act of Sortes." Similarly it does not follow that "Plato is an enemy of Sortes; therefore Plato is a something of Sortes." And yet in all these cases one is arguing from the inferior to the superior, because in the first one is arguing from the term "lord" to the term "substance," in the second from the term "zealot" to the term "something," thirdly from the term "act of

[149]

understanding" to the term "act," fourthly from the term "enemy" to the term "something." The response is that the aforementioned rule frequently does not hold but rather fails when the inferior is posited with an oblique case in the antecedent and the superior is posited with the same oblique case in the consequent.

In the thirteenth place it is argued as follows: It does not follow that "Plato hits Sortes; therefore Plato causally affects Sortes," and yet the term "causally affects" is superior to the term "hits," because to hit anything is to causally affect, for to do anything to external matter is to causally affect it. Furthermore, it does not follow that "Plato understands Sortes; therefore he pays attention to Sortes," and yet the term "pays attention to" is superior to the term "understands," for to understand anything is to pay attention to it. Similarly it does not follow that "The king is attacking the colony; therefore he is performing some action toward the colony," since the term "is performing some action toward" is superior to the term "is attacking." The response is that this rule is not universally true but rather in many cases an exception is permitted when the inferior is constructed with an oblique case in the antecedent and the superior word is constructed with the same in the consequent.

In the fourteenth place it is argued as follows: It does not follow that "Man is a very particular species; therefore animal is a very particular species." One must say that in the case of none of these rules does one argue validly that it is clearly so from the first. For the term "animal," taken materially, is not superior to the term "man," nor is the term "man," taken materially, inferior to the term "animal." Furthermore, the preceding arguments having been solved thus, one must note that the aforementioned fourth rule is principally true when one argues from the inferior which is the entire subject or predicate to its superior, as long as one argues without negation and without a word including negation. For if one argues with a negation or distribution, then the rule is not universally true but rather exceptions are permitted in many cases, as were the above mentioned arguments which we considered.

The fifth rule is this: A consequence which involves arguing from the inferior to the superior with a negation posited subsequently is valid, as for example: "A man is not running; therefore an animal is not running." In the first place one argues against this rule in the following fashion: It does not follow that "Sortes is not an animal; therefore a man is not an animal"; this is obvious, because after the death of Sortes the antecedent is true and the consequent is false; and yet one is arguing here according to the fifth rule with negation posited subsequently. The response is that the rule is understood when one argues with a constant inferior and superior, as for example, it validly follows that: "Sortes is not an animal; and Sortes is not a man; therefore a man is not an animal."

Second, it is argued as follows against the rule: It does not follow that "Only a man is not a non-man; therefore only an animal is not an animal," and yet it is argued according to this rule that it is known that the *non sequitur* is obvious, because, posited the case that men do not exist but other animals do, then the antecedent is true but the consequent is false, as is obvious from the exponents of each. The response is that it is not valid in the case of exclusives. This is obvious because they are equipollent with hypotheticals. One must know that this fifth rule is true when one argues with a constant inferior and superior in categorical propositions.

The sixth rule is the following: An argument from an inferior functioning as predicate to a superior with exclusive words is a valid consequence. For it validly follows that "Sortes is only a man; therefore he is only an animal." Similarly it also follows that "Sortes is only an animal; therefore Sortes is only a substance."

The seventh rule is: An argument from a distributed superior to an inferior is a valid consequence, for example, "Every man runs; therefore Sortes runs." An argument against this rule is as follows: It does not follow that "Every man is an animal; therefore Adam is an animal," and yet one is arguing according to the rule. That it does not follow is obvious, because the antecedent is true and the consequent is false. The response is that a consequence from the superior to an inferior is not valid in affirmatives, unless one argues with a constant subject, because a consequence without a constant subject is not valid, for example, one validly infers: "Every man is an animal; Adam is a man; therefore, Adam is an animal."

Secondly, it is argued as follows: It does not follow that "Sortes is not beginning to be colored; therefore he is not beginning to be white." The answer is that the rule does not hold in the case of the words "begins" and "ceases" which include negation.

The eighth rule is: An argument from an exclusive affirmative to its universal with transposed terms is a valid consequence. And it is noteworthy that I say "with transposed terms" so that that which is the subject in one is the predicate in the other and conversely, because a consequence of such a kind is not valid without a transposition of terms; for example, it does not follow that "Only man runs; therefore every man runs." With transposed terms, the consequence is valid. For it validly follows that "Only man runs; therefore everyone running is a man." It is argued against the rule in the first place as follows, that a *non sequitur* is proved. Let the case be assumed that some man

[151]

runs and that also some ass runs, then it does not follow that "It is not the case that only man runs; therefore everyone running is not a man," yet the antecedent is true and the consequent is false. The response is that this rule does not hold universally in the case of exclusive negative propositions which are expounded affirmatively, as are these: "Only man does not run" and "Only a is not b," because it does not follow formally that "Only a is not b; therefore no a is b," because one is arguing from the non-distributed to the distributed.

Second, it is argued as follows: It does not follow that "Only animal was man; therefore every man was an animal," and yet here one is arguing according to the rule. And that it does not follow is now proved. Posit that now there is the first exception, the being of Sortes. In this way the antecedent is true, namely, "Only animal was man," and the consequent is false, namely, "Every man was an animal." But this is false in this case, because Sortes is or was a man, yet he never was an animal, because he never was according to the case posited. The response to this is, that in order that the rule be true, it is required that a variation of amplification should not occur in the aforementioned argument. For the term "*man*" in the exclusive proposition which is the antecedent is not amplified and consequently one is arguing there from the less extended to the more extended distributively, which consequence is not valid.

Third, it is argued as follows: It does not follow that "It is necessary that only a creator be god; therefore it is necessary that every god be a creator," and yet here one is arguing according to the rule. That it does not follow is obvious, because the antecedent is true and the consequent is false. The response is that the rule permits an exception in the case of modal propositions and especially in the case of necessary ones.

The ninth rule is: An argument from a universal affirmative to its exclusive affirmative with transposed terms is a valid consequence, as "Every man is an animal; therefore only an animal is a man."

The tenth rule is: An argument from an exceptive negative to an exclusive affirmative is a valid consequence, as it validly follows that "No being with the exception of man runs; therefore only man runs." That this consequence is valid is obvious, because the exponents of the consequent follow from the exponents of the antecedent; therefore the consequent follows from the antecedent. It is argued against this rule as follows: It does not follow that "No man with the exception of Sortes runs; therefore only Sortes runs," and yet it is argued according to this rule that a *non sequitur* is proved. For posit the case that Sortes alone may run and one ass runs, then the antecedent is true and the consequent false, as is obvious to anyone examining the ex-

[152]

ponents of each. The response to this is that for the aforementioned rule to be true, it is required that the term taken as excepted be the subject of an exclusive proposition, and that the principal subject of an exceptive proposition or the term from which the exception is made, which is the same, and also the exceptive principal predicate be both placed in an exclusive in the position of the predicate, for example, "No man with the exception of Sortes runs; 'therefore only Sortes is a running man' or 'therefore only Sortes is a man who runs.'" Another example: "No animal with the exception of Sortes has an intellect; therefore only Sortes has an intellect." Another example: "No animal with the exception of Sortes can be beatified; therefore only man is an animal able to be beatified."

The eleventh rule is: An argument from an exceptive affirmative to an exclusive negative is a valid consequence, as it validly follows that "Every being with the exception of God is a creature; therefore only God is not a creature." It is argued against that rule as follows: It does not follow that "Every man with the exception of Sortes runs; therefore only Sortes does not run," yet here one is arguing, according to the rule. That this does not follow is now proved. For posited that every man, who is not Sortes, runs but he himself does not run, then the antecedent is true, as is obvious from the positing, and the consequent is false. And this is obvious, because the second exposition is false, namely, "Everything which is not Sortes runs." The response to this is that for that rule to be universally true, the condition which was expressed concerning the immediately preceding rule is required. But when that condition has been observed, there is a valid consequence. For it validly follows that "Every man with the exception of Sortes runs; therefore only Sortes is a non-running man."

The twelfth rule is: An argument from an exclusive affirmative to to an exceptive negative and from an exclusive negative to an exceptive affirmative is a valid consequence. An example of the first is as follows: It validly follows that "Only man is risible; therefore nothing with the exception of man is risible." An example of the second is as follows: It validly follows that "Only Sortes does not run; therefore every being with the exception of Sortes runs." But it must be known that the one maintaining that twelfth rule has to say as a consequence that the term taken as excepted, namely, that to which the exceptive sign is attached, is not distributed by the exceptive sign. For example, it is necessary to say that in the proposition: "Every animal with the ception of man runs," the term "man" is not distributed but is understood confusedly only. And I believe that this is true. Therefore it is necessary to speak thus in holding that rule, because someone might argue from the non-distributed to the distributed.

The thirteenth rule is this: An argument from an exclusive affirmative to its anteceding proposition is a valid consequence; for example, it validly follows that: "Only man runs; therefore man runs." Similarly it validly follows that "Only man does not run; therefore man does not run." It is argued against this rule as follows: It does not follow that "It is not the case that only man runs; therefore man does not run." The response is that this rule does not hold true in exclusive negatives where negation precedes the exclusive sign.

The fourteenth rule is: An argument from a proposition in which the predicate is posited without an exclusive word to the same predicate repeated with an exclusive word is a valid consequence; for example, it validly follows that "Sortes is a man; therefore Sortes is only a man." Similarly it follows that "Sortes is an animal; therefore Sortes is only an animal." It is argued against this rule as follows: It does not follow that "Sortes is a bachelor; therefore he is only a bachelor," the case that he is a bachelor and a master having been posited, for in this way the antecedent is true and the consequent is false. The response consists in denying that it does not follow. Nay, rather there is a valid consequence in taking the consequent in the composite sense which is fitting from the force of the sentence, since Sortes is only a bachelor. For it is denoted by it that Sortes is not as yet other than a bachelor. But nevertheless that proposition, "Sortes is only a bachelor," sometimes is accustomed to be taken in a general sense, according as the term "only" excludes another degree than the baccalaureate. In taking it thus, it is false in the case posited but it is certain that that second sense is not fitting from the force of the sentence.

The fifteenth rule is: An argument from the things from which an induction is made to the induced is a valid and a formal consequence. An example that validly follows is: "Sortes is an animal; Plato is an animal and so forth; therefore every man is an animal." It is argued against this rule as follows. Posit the case that only three designated men, namely, Sortes and Plato and Cicero exist, and tomorrow more would be born, then the following consequence is not valid: "Sortes runs; Plato runs; Cicero runs; therefore every man runs," and yet one is arguing from the things from which the induction is made to the induced, because one is arguing from the sufficiently enumerated singulars to the universal. And that this does not follow is proved, because tomorrow the antecedent will be true and the consequent false, the case having been posited that those three may run tomorrow but the others who should be born tomorrow may not run. The response consists in conceding that the aforementioned consequence is not valid nor is one arguing according to the rule, because an induction is never sufficiently made unless the closing expression "*and so forth"* or something similar is added to the antecedent, which closing expression having been added, the aforementioned consequence is valid; for it validly follows that "Sortes runs; Plato runs; Cicero runs *and so forth;* therefore every man runs." Similarly that closing expression ought to be added in negatives whenever an induction is made in negative propositions as is obvious in the case: "Sortes does not run; Plato does not run *and so forth;* therefore no man runs."

Second, it is argued as follows: It does not follow that "A man is Sortes; a man is Plato and so forth; therefore a man is every man." The response to this is that there is an invalid induction, because one is arguing from the many determined suppositions of one term to one determined supposition of the same term and that term is not taken in the antecedent with a relative of identity, which however is necessary.

The sixteenth rule is: An argument from "is" appended to a third [term] *(de tertio adiacente)* to "is" appended secondly *(de secundo adiacente)* is a valid consequence, for example, "Man is white; therefore man is." And I call a proposition one "with 'is' appended to a third [term]" *(de tertio adiacente),* [when there is one] in which an explicit predicate is posited, for example, this "is": "Man is an animal"; or [when there is one] in which an adjectival verb which includes a predicate is posited, for example, "A man is running." I call that proposition one "with 'is' appended secondly" *(de secundo adiacente),* [when there is a proposition] in which one posits for the copula the substantive verb "is" or its conjugates or the composite "It is possible that it is" or the composite "It is necessary that it is" or the composite "It is contingent that it is" or the composite "It is impossible that it is" but one does not posit any explicit predicate. For example, the following propositions are [ones] "with 'is' appended secondly" *(de secundo adiacente),* "It is possible that man is," "It is necessary that man is."

It is argued against the rule as follows: It does not follow that "No man is running; therefore no man is," yet one is arguing according to the rule. The answer is that the rule does not hold in the case of negatives. It is argued against the rule in the second place as follows: "Only man is running; therefore only man is." The answer is that the rule does not hold in the case of exclusives, because such propositions virtually include a negative proposition. Third, it is argued as follows: It does not follow that "Aresto is dead; therefore Aresto is." The response is that this rule does not hold universally when the predicates are amplified on account of "is" appended secondly *(de secundo adiacente).* Fourth, it is argued as follows: It does not follow that "Adam is a proper noun; therefore Adam is"; "The antichrist is a singular term; therefore the antichrist is." The response consists in conceding that these consequences are not valid nor are they formed according to the rule mentioned, because the rule is understood concerning exceptive terms with the same supposition but this does not hold in the case of the aforementioned consequences, for in their antecedents the terms "Adam" and "the antichrist" involve material supposition according to the general opinion, whereas in their consequences they involve personal supposition.

The seventeenth rule is: An argument from a copulative whole to one part of it is a valid and formal consequence, as it validly follows that "Sortes is running and Plato is disputing; therefore, Sortes is running." It is argued against the rule as follows: It does not follow that: "God is or a chimaera is and man is an animal; therefore a chimaera is," and yet it appears that one is arguing according to the rule. The response is that the rule is understood when one argues from a copulative whole to one principal part of it but one is not arguing in this way in the example.

The eighteenth rule is: An argument from an extreme copulated as a whole to one part of it is not a valid formal consequence. The rule is proven, for it does not follow that "Sortes and Plato are pulling a ship; therefore Sortes is pulling a ship," posited that both are pulling one ship. It is argued against this rule that it validly follows that "Sortes and Plato are: therefore Sortes is." The response is that that consequence is valid. But it is not formal, because it does not hold in the case of all exactly similar terms, the form of arguing in exactly the same manner having been retained.

The nineteenth rule: An argument from a disjunctive whole taken with the opposite of one part to another part of it which is not destroyed, is a valid consequence and a formal one. An example: It validly follows that "Sortes is running or Plato is arguing; but Sortes is not running; therefore Plato is arguing." One must know, however, that the rule is understood concerning the contradictory opposite but not the contrary or the subalternate or the subcontrary.

The twentieth rule is: An argument from a conditional whole taken with the positing of the antecedent to the positing of the consequent is a valid inference. An example is that it validly follows that "If Sortes is running, Sortes is moved; but Sortes is running; therefore Sortes is moved."

The twenty-first and final rule of the treatise is this: An argument from a conditional whole taken with the contradictory opposite of the consequent to the contradictory opposite of the antecedent is a valid consequence, as it validly follows that "If Sortes is running, Sortes is moved; but Sortes is not moved; therefore Sortes is not running."

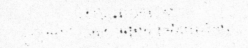